PREFACE

1. Scope

This publication provides fundamental principles and guidance for providing bulk petroleum and water in support of US military operations.

2. Purpose

This publication has been prepared under the direction of the Chairman of the Joint Chiefs of Staff. It sets forth doctrine to govern the joint activities and performance of the Armed Forces of the United States in joint operations and provides the doctrinal basis for interagency coordination and for US military involvement in multinational operations. It provides military guidance for the exercise of authority by combatant commanders and other joint force commanders (JFCs) and prescribes joint doctrine for operations, education, and training. It provides military guidance for use by the Armed Forces in preparing their appropriate plans. It is not the intent of this publication to restrict the authority of the JFC from organizing the force and executing the mission in a manner the JFC deems most appropriate to ensure unity of effort in the accomplishment of the overall objective.

3. Application

a. Doctrine and guidance established in this publication apply to the commanders of combatant commands, subunified commands, joint task forces, and subordinate components of these commands. These principles and guidance also may apply when significant forces of one Service are attached to forces of another Service or when significant forces of one Service support forces of another Service.

b. The guidance in this publication is authoritative; as such, this doctrine will be followed except when, in the judgment of the commander, exceptional circumstances dictate otherwise. If conflicts arise between the contents of this publication and the contents of Service publications, this publication will take precedence for the activities of joint forces unless the Chairman of the Joint Chiefs of Staff, normally in coordination with the other members of the Joint Chiefs of Staff, has provided more current and specific guidance. Commanders of forces operating as part of a multinational (alliance or coalition) military command should follow multinational doctrine and procedures ratified by the United States. For doctrine and procedures not ratified by the United States, commanders should evaluate and follow the multinational command's doctrine and procedures, where applicable and consistent with US law, regulations, and doctrine.

For the Chairman of the Joint Chiefs of Staff:

WILLIAM E. GORTNEY
VADM, USN
Director, Joint Staff

Intentionally Blank

SUMMARY OF CHANGES
REVISION OF JOINT PUBLICATION 4-03
DATED 23 MAY 2003

- **This document is substantially revised and the entire publication should be reviewed for detailed changes**

- **New table of contents parallels Joint Publication (JP) 4-0, *Joint Logistics***

- **Updates graphics to reflect latest doctrinal changes and introduce contemporary content**

- **Provides current quotes and examples (incorporating Haiti, Desert Storm/Desert Shield, Operation IRAQI FREEDOM/Operation ENDURING FREEMDOM content)**

- **Expands bulk petroleum discussion into five (vice three) chapters**

- **Significantly reinforces the importance of standardization, flexibility, and interoperability**

- **Delineates combatant commander responsibilities with respect to the single fuel concept**

- **Elaborates on core capabilities**

- **Discusses bulk petroleum in terms of planning, executing, and controlling**

- **Introduces the Joint Logistics Environment and the Joint Operating Framework**

- **Introduces the Bulk Petroleum Common Operational Picture**

- **Clarifies Title 10, United States Code, responsibilities**

- **Eliminates mature and immature theater and aligns content to modularity concepts in JP 3-0, *Joint Operations***

- **Discusses additional considerations for quality, environment, and contracting**

- **Adds the responsibilities for a subarea petroleum office, established by the joint petroleum office, to fulfill petroleum logistics requirements in support of the joint force commander**

- **Expands and updates water support operations**

- **Adds a scenario-based appendix, Appendix C, "Petroleum Scenario," with solution to reinforce concepts within the publication**

Intentionally Blank

TABLE OF CONTENTS

CHAPTER V
CONTROLLING JOINT BULK PETROLEUM LOGISTICS

CHAPTER VI
PRINCIPLES OF BULK WATER PURIFICATION, STORAGE, AND
DISTRIBUTION

APPENDIX

GLOSSARY

FIGURE

Intentionally Blank

EXECUTIVE SUMMARY
COMMANDER'S OVERVIEW

- **Discusses joint bulk petroleum concepts and principles**

- **Explains how the complex nature of the joint logistics environment will determine how bulk petroleum support is delivered to the joint forces**

- **Covers core joint bulk petroleum capabilities**

- **Describes planning and execution for joint bulk petroleum logistics**

- **Discusses the control of joint bulk petroleum logistics**

- **Outlines responsibilities at each level of authority**

- **Conveys the need to take advantage of host nation support whenever possible**

- **Describes the principles of bulk water purification, storage, and distribution**

Joint Bulk Petroleum Overview

Bulk petroleum, a common supply item, presents a significant logistical challenge when moving, storing, and distributing.

Providing forces with the right fuel, in the right place, and at the right time involves determining peacetime and wartime requirements, contracting and allocating product, arranging for bulk storage, moving products forward to and within the theater, ensuring quality control, issuing and accounting for the fuel, and maintaining distribution equipment and facilities.

Concept of joint bulk petroleum operations.

Providing bulk petroleum support to joint operations requires the Services to develop complementary tactical distribution systems and the Defense Logistics Agency (DLA) to provide common products to the combatant commands (CCMDs) and Services. The nature of joint bulk petroleum support will vary depending on the commercial development of the theater, and whether force employment is single-Service, joint, or multinational. However, the Department of Defense (DOD) goal is a single-fuel concept (SFC). An SFC has benefits; one fuel is considerably easier to manage than multiple fuels, allowing the functions of fuel storage, transportation, and distribution to be tailored for maximum efficiency.

Principles of joint bulk petroleum.	Bulk petroleum requires special handling and storage, and has a demand significantly larger than other supply classes. For these reasons, any viable support concept must incorporate the **principles of standardization, flexibility, and interoperability.**
Standardization.	DOD components should continue to minimize the number of bulk petroleum products that must be stocked and distributed, plan to use fuels readily available worldwide, and minimize the military-unique characteristics of DOD fuels.
Flexibility.	Military systems and support equipment capable of using alternate fuels, to include kerosene-based products and ultra-low sulfur diesel, provide the joint force commander (JFC) with opportunities to increase storage and distribution efficiency while reducing cost, including the demands for security (threat or environmental based).
Interoperability.	Interoperable fuel handling equipment and connectors between components and, when possible, multinational forces, allow for more timely distribution and support with greater efficiency, including a reduction in the number of deployed systems operating within the theater.
The Nation's ability to project and sustain military power depends on effective joint logistics.	Joint bulk petroleum logistics requires the combined efforts of a number of civilian, military, and commercial organizations. DOD joint petroleum logistics supply chain is a global network that delivers bulk petroleum critical to the joint force. The goal of this supply chain is to maximize force readiness while optimizing the allocation of petroleum resources. Logisticians must manage the petroleum supply chain to link separate global operations spanning all levels of war.
The complex nature of the joint logistics environment (JLE) will determine how bulk petroleum support is delivered to the joint forces.	Sustained logistics readiness in the joint logistics environment (JLE) depends on a collaborative network of relationships throughout the operational environment and at all levels of command. The geographic combatant commanders (GCCs) have the primary function of planning, executing, and controlling bulk

petroleum support in their areas of responsibility (AORs), across strategic, operational, and tactical levels.

Strategic level.

At the strategic level, the combination of Service, agency, and commercial organizations constitutes the backbone of joint bulk petroleum logistics, which aid in the projection and long-term sustainment of the combatant commander's (CCDR's) joint bulk petroleum requirements.

Operational level.

At the operational level, the joint bulk petroleum logistician integrates strategic and tactical capabilities of the joint forces to meet the CCMD's operational requirements. The joint bulk petroleum logistician encounters the greatest challenges at this level because of the difficulty in integrating the capabilities from many providers who must project, distribute, and sustain bulk petroleum for the JFC.

Tactical level.

At the tactical level, the responsibility to install and operate tactical petroleum storage and distribution systems usually lies with the Services. The Services derive their sustainment primarily from the strategic and operational levels for bulk petroleum operations and leverage the benefits of that sustainment to permit freedom of action. The joint bulk petroleum logistician contributes to joint force readiness by applying the three imperative capabilities critical to success: unity of effort, JLE-wide visibility, and rapid and precise response.

Core Joint Petroleum Logistics Capabilities

Theater bulk petroleum operations revolve around a push-pull supply system.

Landbased customers request fuel from the Army component's theater sustainment command (TSC), another Service component organization, or an agency assigned as the lead Service for bulk petroleum support. The TSC normally includes a petroleum section and a distribution management center. The petroleum section is tasked to manage and account for theater bulk petroleum. It also coordinates tactical petroleum operations and quality surveillance (QS) of bulk petroleum in the theater. The distribution management center schedules movement of product forward into the support area based on a combination of available storage, distribution assets, and anticipated customer demands.

Petroleum support for maritime forces.

Bulk petroleum support for maritime forces is similar to that discussed above; however, sea-based customers interact more directly with terminal operators at defense fuel support points (DFSPs).

Basic stockage concept.

The basic stockage concept in theater operations is to have sufficient storage to support the most demanding operation plan (OPLAN), and keep fuel on-hand inventories at or near maximum authorized levels, while using available transportation assets as efficiently as possible.

Effective and efficient supply operations enable the projection and sustainment of joint bulk petroleum in the theater.

Effective, efficient, and sustained joint bulk petroleum support is achieved by integrating Service, agency, and other capabilities. DLA Energy supports this goal by exercising strategic-level management responsibilities for consolidation and review of requirements, procurement, funding, budgeting, storage, and designated distribution of bulk petroleum to meet the operational requirements.

Today's world is highly dependent upon petroleum products. Therefore, it is likely that some infrastructure would be available for use by US forces almost anywhere in the world. However, it is entirely likely, depending on the size of the operation, that sufficient in-place and operational fuel storage, on-hand product, road networks, rail lines, and easily traversed lines of communications (LOCs) would not exist to support planned operations. Therefore, tactical systems may be required to supplement infrastructure available in the theater.

Bulk petroleum received via joint logistics over-the-shore.

Bulk petroleum may need to be received via joint logistics over-the-shore (JLOTS) operations. Such operations use an offshore petroleum discharge system (OPDS) or other bulk liquids transfer system to deliver fuel to tactical storage facilities located immediately ashore. The offshore system delivers fuel to a tactical or commercial terminal normally operated by a tactical pipeline and terminal operating unit. Fuel may then be moved forward through the use of trucks, rail, or installed pipeline systems that can quickly establish inland product distribution. If the theater is not an active theater of war, it should have an established peacetime operating stocks (POS) level and petroleum war reserve requirements.

The joint petroleum offices (JPOs), at the direction of the Chairman of the Joint Chiefs of Staff, submit two key joint petroleum reports: bulk petroleum contingency report and bulk petroleum capabilities report.

The **bulk petroleum contingency report** (REPOL) provides the Joint Staff, Services, and DLA Energy with summary information on bulk petroleum inventories, a damage assessment for bulk petroleum distribution systems, and other strategic information pertaining to bulk petroleum support posture at specific bases, posts, locations, and/or forward operating bases, etc. The REPOL is widely used by the Service components, DLA Energy, joint petroleum office (JPO), and subarea petroleum office (SAPO) to manage theater resupply and distribution requirements and critical actions affecting theater petroleum distribution. The **bulk petroleum capabilities report** provides the Joint Staff, Services, and DLA Energy with an assessment of bulk petroleum support capabilities for contingency requirements in a specific theater.

Quality management of bulk petroleum is essential to ensure bulk petroleum products are suitable for their intended use.

The physical characteristics and complex chemical makeup of bulk petroleum products necessitates vigilance in quality management at the strategic, operational, and tactical levels. Sediment and water are the most common types of contaminants found in storage, distribution, and dispensing systems. Their presence can cause serious problems in fuel systems, particularly in aircraft. Positive action must be taken to prevent and eliminate the occurrence of these contaminants in bulk products.

Fuel safety.

Safety is a principal concern. Petroleum products are hazardous due to their toxicity, explosiveness, flammability, and potential to create environmental damage. Prescribed safety precautions will be strictly followed for the protection of personnel, equipment, and the environment.

Environmental concerns.

All US military activities are required to conform to US environmental laws and guidelines as set forth in DOD directives. Leaks or spills must be avoided to prevent the discharge of petroleum products to waterways and underground water tables.

Defense Logistics Agency (DLA) Energy has responsibility for the centralized procurement of bulk petroleum for Department of Defense.

Contracting is commonly used to augment organic military and other sources of support such as multinational logistic support and host-nation support (HNS), but contracting is often not properly planned for or integrated into the overall JFC logistics support effort. Contracting support capabilities should be considered when needed to augment organic support capabilities and in situations where acquisition and cross-servicing agreement or HNS agreements do not exist or when these agreements cannot provide sufficient bulk petroleum products.

Planning for Joint Bulk Petroleum Logistics

The DLA Energy regional offices and Service components support the JPO in developing a practical, sustainable petroleum support concept and plan.

The supported CCDR's JPO is responsible for the overall planning of petroleum logistic support for joint operations within the assigned AOR. This planning occurs at the strategic level and usually is embodied in the petroleum appendix to the logistics annex of the military OPLANs or concept plans.

Joint bulk petroleum plan development involves meticulous attention to the ability of global partners to provide bulk petroleum assets to the theater. The scope of this planning is widespread and involves the ability of contracting partners and host nations (HNs) to complement the global partners' strategic capabilities. Plan development must also integrate the availability of secure LOCs, the intensity of current and future operations, and the organizational structure of the JFC.

Required actions when planning for bulk petroleum operations.

Project accurate, timely fuel requirements, maximize use of in-country civilian or HNS fuel facilities, tailor fuel equipment and support packages to the requirement, standardize and ensure compatibility of fuel equipment to support joint and multinational fuel operations, establish the theater JPO or subarea fuel manager with assistance provided by DLA Energy regional offices and Service components.

One critical aspect of joint bulk petroleum planning is the infrastructure where the operation will be conducted.

Some theaters will have HN assets available, such as pipelines, storage facilities, and railways, that will help support the bulk petroleum distribution system. In these situations, airbases, tactical airfields, and other sites can be supported by pipelines whenever tactically feasible. In other theaters, HN or commercial bulk petroleum facilities may not be available and tactical assets will need to be used. Tactical bulk petroleum supply systems may include limited tanker mooring systems, floating hose lines, submarine pipelines, inland tank farms, temporary overland hose lines or pipelines, and collapsible tanks.

Factors for computing peacetime operating stocks.

The fuel POS levels are computed annually by DLA Energy for all DFSPs and utilize the following factors:

Daily Demand Rate – The past and projected years' issues are used to calculate a daily demand rate.

Economic Resupply Quantity – The fuel quantity a defense fuel support point can receive that ideally balances economic and operational requirements.

Safety Level – The safety level is the amount of fuel to compensate for variability in resupply time and demand during the resupply cycle.

Unobtainable Inventory – That fuel needed to prime a storage dispensing system such as pipeline fill, manifold fill, and tank bottom below the suction line.

Planning considerations.

Plans should consider at least the following points: mission, fuel requirements, infrastructure, equipment, support units, assumptions, command/control, responsibilities, quality, interoperability of fuel, transfer systems, sustainability and survivability, theater-specific factors, threat environment, limiting factors, and sealift and other distribution methods.

Executing Bulk Petroleum Logistics

The goal of bulk petroleum support is to fulfill the requirements of the combatant commander's (CCDR's) concept of operations and intent.

The transition from planning to execution can occur abruptly, in phases, or even concurrently. The framework for bulk petroleum support calls for a joint staff organization with clearly defined roles and responsibilities for both the organic joint staff and the augmented component that provides specialized support.

DOD bulk petroleum inventories consist of pre-positioned war reserve stocks and POS. They take into account economic resupply, safety levels, unobtainable inventory, and deliberate planning requirements.

The established infrastructure within a theater supports the supply and distribution of bulk petroleum. Stocks are moved from secure military or commercial sources to forward areas and terminals as demand or plans require. The movement and redistribution of assets are accomplished through a joint effort involving the CCMDs, Service components, and DLA Energy, interfacing with US Transportation Command (USTRANSCOM) components for product movement outside the operational area.

Actual procedures to accomplish the delivery of products to the end user depend on the sources of product and the conditions in the operational area.

The theater normally has some HN assets available or theater support contracts (i.e., fuel sources, terminal facilities, pipelines, railways, and trucks) that should be used to the maximum extent possible to help offset US requirements. Because the capabilities of allies or coalition partners are theater unique, the JPO or SAPO is responsible for assessing these potential capabilities and integrating them into appropriate plans and operations.

Pipeline distribution.

Pipelines are often the most economical and effective method of inland fuel distribution. Bulk petroleum is generally most efficiently moved from base terminals and rear storage locations to the combat zone by pipelines. A fully developed theater fuel distribution system may include ship discharge ports (with moorings and piping manifolds), seaside and inland fuel storage tanks, pump stations, and pipelines.

Truck distribution.

In many cases, truck distribution may offer the tactical commander more flexibility in the distribution of fuel.

Tactical systems.

A tactical tank farm consisting of collapsible tanks is constructed at airbases or other locations and connected to the main hose line or pipeline. The airbases or other locations then employ tactical servicing systems that have hoses, pumps, and filters to issue the product to the end user. Bulk petroleum may need to be received via JLOTS operations to deliver fuel to tactical storage facilities located immediately ashore. The OPDS delivers fuel to a tactical or commercial terminal normally operated by a tactical pipeline and terminal operating unit.

Air delivery.

When LOCs are not secure or when operating in noncontiguous areas, Service component aircraft carrying fuel trucks, collapsible tanks, 500-gallon collapsible drums, or 55-gallon drums may be required to distribute fuel. Currently, aerial bulk fuel delivery system enables cargo aircraft to transport from 3,000 to 30,000 gallons of fuel to the tactical storage and issue systems.

Other distribution.

The pipeline system may be supplemented by other means of bulk delivery, such as barges, rail tank cars, aircraft, bulk truck transports, and commercial distribution equipment provided by the host.

Consideration must be given to theater-specific factors such as available commercial and host nation supply sources and transportation assets. Many of these sources of petroleum supply will have political, technical, and economic factors that limit their availability.

Some factors that commanders and planners must take into consideration include the following: force protection for contractor personnel, fuel equipment, and stocks; contractor limitations with regard to support; contractor required logistic support; regional capabilities and intermediate staging bases to support strategic airlift transiting through the AOR; regional capabilities to support Air Force tankers supporting air cap operations; airfield limitations, maximum number of aircraft an airfield can have on the ground; LOC capabilities and limitations; and specialty fuel requirements.

Threat environment.

While theater-specific factors may require force protection actions for contractor personnel, petroleum equipment, and stocks, quality assurance (QA) actions should also be considered. Ensuring adequate security may include specific and appropriate countermeasures against tampering, adulteration, substitution, contamination, and other actions that could make the fuel unusable or potentially damaging to the end user.

Military construction; sustainment, restoration, and modernization; and environmental compliance.

DLA, through DLA Energy, shall establish and maintain a DOD bulk petroleum distribution system and related programs in coordination with the Services and the CCMDs. DLA, Services, and CCMDs have interrelated responsibilities to plan and execute for military construction; minor construction; operation of facilities; sustainment, restoration, and modernization;

and environmental compliance of bulk storage and distribution facilities in support of the bulk petroleum management mission.

Concluding joint bulk petroleum logistics operations.

It is important for joint logistics to monitor these transitional activities and ensure logistical resources used for the completed actions are given new tasks or the resources are redeployed back to home station.

Controlling Joint Bulk Petroleum Logistics

The ability of the joint bulk petroleum logistician to synchronize outcomes within the JLE presents serious challenges.

Control of joint logistics requires organizing staff and operational level logisticians around their abilities to assist in planning and executing joint logistics support operations. It also involves integrating and synchronizing responsibilities, designating lead Service responsibilities, and developing procedures to optimize joint logistic outcomes.

The integrated materiel management concept underlies the principles in joint bulk petroleum doctrine.

Integrated materiel management (IMM) is normally used when a single DOD agency has total management responsibility for supplying a specific product or group of related items to the Armed Forces of the United States. Because IMM both supports and influences this doctrine's usage and interpretation, an understanding of its conception is important.

Under Secretary of Defense for Acquisition, Technology, and Logistics.

The **Under Secretary of Defense for Acquisition, Technology, and Logistics** is responsible for establishing policies for management of bulk petroleum stocks and facilities, and providing guidance to other DOD agencies, Joint Staff, and Services.

Chairman of the Joint Chiefs of Staff.

The **Chairman of the Joint Chiefs of Staff** coordinates with DLA Energy, Services, and CCMDs to resolve petroleum issues. The **logistics directorate of the Joint Staff (J-4)** is the primary agent of the Chairman of the Joint Chiefs of Staff for all bulk petroleum matters. Key responsibilities of the J-4 that influence joint petroleum principles and affect operations are: act as the focal point for joint bulk petroleum doctrine; make recommendations to DOD on wartime fuel sourcing and pre-positioning days of supply (DOS); prescribe CCMD procedures for reporting bulk petroleum; and provide fuel inputs to the Joint Strategic

Capabilities Plan and review fuels planning in prescribed joint OPLANs.

Geographic combatant commander/JPO.

The **GCC** has the predominant fuels responsibility within a theater, and this responsibility is discharged by the JPO. The **JPO** works in conjunction with its Service components, SAPOs, and DLA Energy to plan, coordinate, and oversee all phases of bulk petroleum support for US forces and other organizations, as directed, and employed or planned for possible employment in the theater.

Subarea petroleum office.

A **SAPO** is a sub-office of a JPO and is established by the CCDR or JFC (usually upon JPO recommendation) to fulfill bulk petroleum planning and execution matters in a section of the theater for which the JPO is responsible.

Services.

Each **Service** provides for product handling at its operational locations. The Services coordinate all fuel issues with the appropriate JPO, SAPO, and DLA Energy during single-Service, joint, and multinational operations, including exercises and deployments, to ensure efficiency and avoid duplication of effort. Normally the Army will provide distribution of bulk petroleum within theater. When required, and if the equipment assets are available, other Services may be tasked to supplement (or assume) the theater bulk petroleum distribution mission.

Army.

The Army normally provides management of overland petroleum support, including inland waterways, to US land-based forces of all DOD components.

Air Force.

The Air Force shall maintain the capability to provide tactical support to Air Force units at improved and austere locations. It shall also provide distribution of bulk petroleum products by air where immediate support is needed at remote locations.

Navy.

The Navy shall provide seaward and over-the-shore bulk petroleum products to the high-water mark for US sea- and land-based forces of all DOD components. It shall maintain the capability to provide bulk petroleum support to naval forces afloat and ashore (to include US Coast Guard forces assigned to DOD).

Marine Corps.	The Marine Corps shall maintain a capability to provide bulk petroleum support to Marine Corps units.
Coast Guard.	The Coast Guard shall coordinate petroleum requirements with the Navy.
DLA.	The Director, DLA, is responsible for meeting designated petroleum support requirements of the DOD components. These functional responsibilities have been delegated to the Director, DLA Energy, and include procurement, ownership, QA and QS, accountability, budgeting, and distribution of bulk petroleum stocks to the point-of-sale.
DLA Energy.	DLA Energy manages the bulk petroleum supply chain from source of supply to the point of customer acceptance as the DOD executive agent (EA) and IMM for bulk petroleum. These responsibilities mandate that DLA Energy exercise total DOD-level management responsibility for bulk petroleum, including the requirements, funding, budgeting, storing, issuing, cataloging, standardizing, and procuring functions.
The JPO, US Transportation Command (USTRANSCOM), represents Commander, USTRANSCOM, on all petroleum and water-related issues involving USTRANSCOM and components.	The Commander, USTRANSCOM, shall plan for and provide air, land, and sea transportation of fuels for DOD during peacetime and wartime. These efforts will supplement and not replace the primary responsibilities assigned to the Services and DLA, especially with regard to intratheater and inland fuel movement and distribution.
	CCMDs should make maximum use of HN and theater support contracted capabilities to meet peacetime and wartime requirements, particularly when logistic support from US units or equipment may not be readily available, when combat forces have outpaced integral logistics capability, or when acquisition of logistics support using these vehicles is more efficient or advantageous to the government. Several different agreements, such as North Atlantic Treaty Organization standardized agreements, defense cooperation agreements, bilateral agreements, implementing arrangements, foreign assistance acts, foreign military sales programs, and reimbursement for multinational

support, may serve CCDRs' and Service components' needs, depending on the degree and type of support required and the specific HN.

Contracts and agreements.

Blanket purchase agreement (BPA). A BPA should be considered for filling anticipated repetitive needs for supplies or services for a stated time period. Individual BPA purchases shall not exceed the simplified acquisition threshold, with the exception of commercial item purchases, which may be substantially larger.

Bunker contracts. These contracts are similar to into-plane contracts and are used for frequent refueling of ships at commercial ports where DLA Energy has no DFSP.

Direct delivery and post camp and station (PC&S) contracts and transportation tenders. DLA Energy, as the EA for worldwide petroleum support, can establish a variety of free on board origin and destination direct delivery PC&S contracts, and transportation tenders to support the CCDR.

HNs, through agreements, can provide a variety of environmental services, while the JFC is expected to comply to the maximum extent with local laws and regulations.

Principles of Bulk Water Purification, Storage, and Distribution

Water is one of the largest and most important life-sustainment commodities.

As water requirements rise above individual or small unit needs, they need to be handled in "bulk" form. Bulk handling calls for special equipment, product-handling safeguards, and standing operating procedures. Interestingly, bulk water is still foraged for on the modern battlefield.

Commanders and their staffs at all levels must be concerned about maintaining water support to allow completion of the unit's mission.

To ensure adequate support, commanders and their staffs should address planning for tactical water support in all plans and orders. Water is supplied as either a packaged or bulk product. A packaged product is manufactured and procured, stored, transported, and supplied in a container. Water in larger quantities is a bulk commodity. Packaged methods require extensive shipping, require materials handling equipment to move, and provide a reduced throughput capability when compared with bulk operations. Planners should weigh the advantages and disadvantages of packaged and bulk water carefully to ensure the best method is chosen to support the contingency.

Tactical bulk water support operations are implemented to purify water as close to the user as possible.

This methodology involves detailed planning for the water point selection site and the purification, storage, and distribution of bulk water. **Bulk water support normally is a Service responsibility.** However, during joint operations, if delegated authority by the GCC, the subordinate JFC may assign water support responsibilities on an area basis using the "lead-Service methodology," i.e., the dominant user or the most capable Service in an area may be tasked to provide water support to all forces operating in that area.

In most situations, water distribution is the "weak link" of the water support system.

Moving water from the production and storage sites to the user can be equipment and manpower intensive. Joint forces must make efficient use of all available assets in conducting water distribution operations.

Water support planning is a continual process that begins with the identification of the force size and planned deployment rate. Time-phased water requirements are then determined and units are selected and scheduled for deployment based on the requirements.

Total water requirements are placed in the theater "water distribution plan" developed by the CCDR, with support from the Service component commander

Critical water support planning elements are: development of detailed water distribution plans; identification of water support requirements for other Services, multinational forces, and HN labor forces; water support structure (personnel and equipment) that is capable of providing the required water production, purification, storage, and distribution; water quality procedures; identification of quality local water; and identification of possible impact on production due to water quality.

Water requirements may vary daily.

Water requirements will depend upon the environment, the tactical situation, and the size of the force. Some requirements, such as cooking, may be indefinite while others may only be for a specific period of time.

Water consumption requirements are based on the size of the force. Water consumption also depends on the region.

Water sources normally are abundant in temperate, arctic, and tropical regions. Although non-potable water is easily available, treatments may be required for certain or all uses. For this reason, non-potable water should be included in consumption estimates if treatment is necessary. **In arid regions, water sources are sparse and water must be transported forward.** In arid regions, in early phases of establishing base camps or forward operating bases, requirements for both potable and non-potable water will be met with potable water in order to prevent having two separate water systems. As a result, total potable requirements will increase in the arid regions.

Several computations must be made to determine supply, purification, and storage requirements for water.

Supply requirement. To compute the total daily water requirement of the force, multiply the actual strength by the proper consumption factor found in the Services' water consumption planning guides.

Purification requirement. To determine the amount of purification equipment needed to support the daily requirement, divide the total daily requirement by the daily production capability of one purification unit.

Storage requirement. Temperate, tropical, and arctic regions usually do not require large amounts of water to be stored. Raw water sources may be adequate to meet non-potable requirements, and the potable requirements can be met by the water purification unit's organic storage tanks. In arid regions, large quantities of potable water must be stored. The storage requirement is based on resupply times, daily requirements, and the DOS requirements established by the commander. In arctic regions, the storage of water may be complicated by freezing temperatures.

Essential consumption.

When enough potable water cannot be produced to meet all the requirements, all but essential consumption must be reduced. **Essential water requirements include drinking, personal hygiene, field feeding, medical treatment, heat casualty treatment, personal contamination control, and patient/equipment decontamination in chemical, biological, radiological, and nuclear (CBRN) environments and, in arid regions, vehicle and aircraft maintenance.**

Water vulnerability assessment.	Vulnerability of the water system to CBRN attack, conventional attack, and man-made/natural hazards must be considered. Normally, a water vulnerability assessment of potential and existing water sources and distribution systems is conducted to evaluate the level of risk. Ensuring adequate security may include specific and appropriate countermeasures against tampering, adulteration, substitution, contamination, and other actions that could make the water unusable or potentially damaging to the end user.
Water support operations.	Water support operations consist of water purification, water storage, water distribution, and other considerations.
Phase I, water purification.	Once an adequate water source has been identified and located, water purification is the first phase of tactical water support operations. During the purification phase, water is drawn from a source and purified to potable standards. Potable water is certified safe for human consumption.
Phase II, water storage.	Water storage is the second phase of water support operations. Storage is normally done at or very close to the purification sites. The goal of water storage is to keep a sufficient quantity on hand to prevent a water shortage if several purification units become non-operational at one time.
Phase III, water distribution.	**Water distribution often is the critical link in water support operations.** It is important that units organize so they will have sufficient organic water distribution equipment to provide supply point distribution. Units must have enough water distribution capacity to supply minimum requirements for water while making only one trip to the water point per day.
Other considerations.	Planners should maximize the use of HN sources if possible. Water planners should assume no HN potable water is available in arid regions. In the early stages of deployment, HN processed or bottled water may be used if it has been certified as potable by preventive medicine personnel.

CONCLUSION

This publication provides fundamental principles and guidance for providing bulk petroleum and water in support of US military operations.

Intentionally Blank

CHAPTER I
JOINT BULK PETROLEUM OVERVIEW

"No matter how well fed, equipped, or officered, without oil and gasoline the modern army is a hopeless monster, mired and marked for destruction."

T.H. Vail Motter (1901–1969), US Army Historian

1. Introduction

a. Bulk petroleum, a common supply item, presents a significant logistical challenge when moving, storing, and distributing. In this publication, all references to petroleum include not only the naturally derived product but also alternative/renewable and synthetic fuels and their blends. **Providing forces with the right fuel, in the right place, and at the right time** involves determining peacetime and wartime requirements, contracting and allocating product, arranging for bulk storage, moving products forward to and within the theater, ensuring quality control, issuing and accounting for the fuel, and maintaining distribution equipment and facilities.

b. International concerns and agreements about air pollution and climate change precipitated significant changes in laws governing fuel specifications and engine emission standards among all industrialized nations. Within the United States, military equipment and fuels are exempt from several laws and regulations. However, the Department of Defense (DOD) has been directly impacted by these statutes governing the public and commercial sectors to meet engine design and gasoline specifications that require unleaded gasoline and ultra-low sulfur diesel (ULSD). The collective impact of these statutory and regulatory changes could affect DOD's ability to achieve broad application of the single-fuel concept (SFC) as experienced in recent operations.

2. Concept of Joint Bulk Petroleum Operations

a. Providing bulk petroleum support to joint operations requires the Services to develop complementary tactical distribution systems and the Defense Logistics Agency (DLA) to provide common products to the combatant commands (CCMDs) and Services. The nature of joint bulk petroleum support will vary depending on the commercial development of the theater, and whether force employment is single-Service, joint, or multinational. However, the DOD goal is an SFC. An SFC has benefits; one fuel is considerably easier to manage than multiple fuels, allowing the functions of fuel storage, transportation, and distribution to be tailored for maximum efficiency. Using JP8 as the single fuel has enhanced long-term storage stability, improved cold weather vehicle operation, reduced engine combustion component wear, and reduced fuel system corrosion problems. In addition, using a single fuel lessens the possibility of dispensing the wrong fuel.

b. Land-based customers request fuel from the Army component's theater sustainment command (TSC) or another Service component or agency assigned as the lead for bulk petroleum support. These organizations schedule movement of product forward from the sustainment base based on a combination of available storage and anticipated customer demands. Sea-based customers essentially perform the same functions, but interact more directly with terminal operators at defense fuel support points (DFSPs). The basic stockage concept in theater operations is to have sufficient storage to support the most demanding operation plan (OPLAN) and keep on-hand inventories at or near maximum authorized levels, while using available transportation assets as efficiently as possible.

3. Principles of Joint Bulk Petroleum

Bulk petroleum requires special handling and storage, and has a demand significantly larger than other supply classes. For these reasons, any viable support concept must incorporate the principles of standardization, flexibility, and interoperability (see Figure I-1).

a. Standardization. DOD components should continue to minimize the number of bulk petroleum products that must be stocked and distributed, plan to use fuels readily available worldwide, and minimize the military-unique characteristics of DOD fuels. Limiting military-unique characteristics allows the use of kerosene-based products for land-based forces, and potentially increases operational flexibility because these fuels are commercially available worldwide. Joint force commanders (JFCs) should attempt to minimize unnecessary fuel type usage when planning for contingencies.

b. Flexibility. Military systems and support equipment capable of using alternate fuels, to include kerosene-based products and ULSD, provide the JFC with opportunities to increase storage and distribution efficiency while reducing cost, including the demands for security (threat or environmental based).

c. Interoperability. Interoperable fuel handling equipment and connectors between components and, when possible, multinational forces (MNFs), allow for more timely distribution and support with greater efficiency, including a reduction in the number of deployed systems operating within the theater. It is also important in multinational operations, where one nation may be designated as the role specialist nation for petroleum logistics. Consequently, to foster interoperability, DOD fuel handling equipment must be of common or compatible design, material, and size.

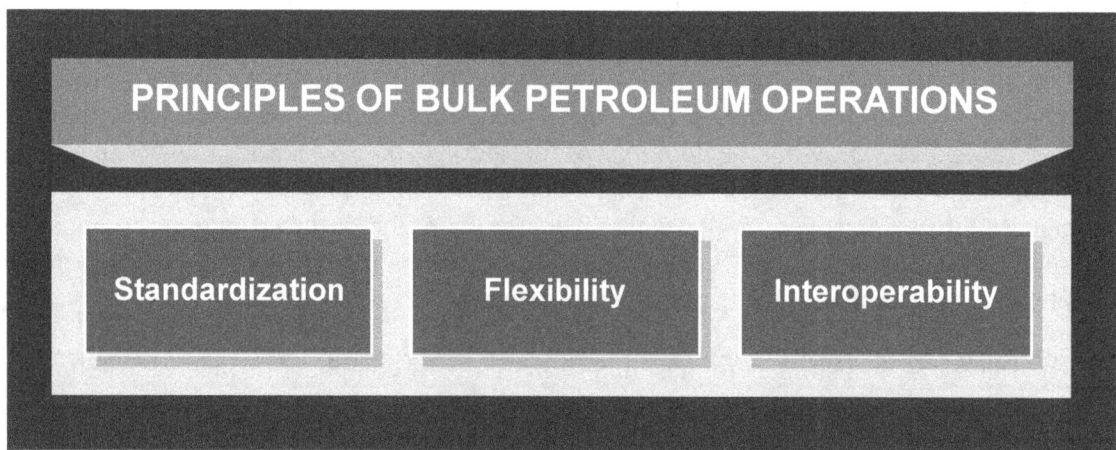

Figure I-1. Principles of Joint Bulk Petroleum Operations

PETROLEUM INTEROPERABILITY

"During Operation DESERT SHIELD, the most difficult part of the early petroleum resupply effort was the actual offloading of fuel from commercial tank trucks. Because the fittings that attached hoses to the trucks were not standardized, we needed special couplings to mate US equipment with Saudi commercial trucks. A similar problem had been resolved in Europe, but the fitting used there would not work in Saudi Arabia. During the early days, a field-expedient procedure was necessary to offload fuel from tankers. Finally, a prototype coupling was assembled. This coupling was purchased locally in sufficient quantities to cover a few early requirements."

Logistics Planning for Desert Storm, *Army Logistician*,
January–February 1991

4. Joint Bulk Petroleum Logistics

a. The Nation's ability to project and sustain military power depends on effective joint logistics. Joint logistics delivers sustained logistic readiness for the combatant commander (CCDR) and subordinate JFCs through the integration of national, multinational, Service, and combat support agency (CSA) capabilities. The integration of these capabilities ensures forces are physically available and properly equipped, at the right place and time, to support the joint force. Joint logisticians coordinate sustained logistic readiness through the integrating functions of planning, executing, and controlling joint logistic operations.

b. Joint logistics is the coordinated use, synchronization, and sharing of two or more Military Departments' logistic resources to support the joint force. From a national perspective, it can be thought of as the ability to project and sustain a logistically ready joint force through the sharing of DOD, interagency, and industrial resources. In today's operational environment, it will include resources from multinational partners, intergovernmental organizations (IGOs), and nongovernmental organizations (NGOs). This provides the JFC the freedom of action necessary to meet mission objectives, which is an essential component of joint operations because the Services seldom have sufficient independent capability to support a joint force. By purposefully combining capabilities, the commander can optimize the allocation of limited resources to provide maximum flexibility to the joint force. This kind of interdependence, focused on common outcomes, delivers sustained logistic readiness.

c. Joint bulk petroleum logistics requires the combined efforts of a number of civilian, military, and commercial organizations. DOD joint petroleum logistics supply chain is a global network that delivers bulk petroleum critical to the joint force. The goal of this supply chain is to maximize force readiness while optimizing the allocation of petroleum resources. Logisticians must manage the petroleum supply chain to link separate global operations spanning all levels of war. The component commands determine bulk petroleum requirements for submission to the CCDR's joint petroleum office (JPO) or subarea petroleum office (SAPO). The JPO or SAPO validates the bulk petroleum requirements for planning and support purposes and provides them to DLA Energy for sourcing, analysis, and development of a support plan in accordance with (IAW) the Joint Operation Planning and

Execution System. As specified in the logistics supplement to the Joint Strategic Capabilities Plan (JSCP), DLA Energy, as a field activity of DLA and executive agent (EA) for bulk petroleum, shall provide "planning products" in support of the CCDR's OPLANs and concept plans (CONPLANs). The concept of operations (CONOPS) for contingency, sourcing analysis of planned time-phased contingency requirements, and logistics supportability analysis (LSA) outlines the risks and feasibility of support from the industry supplier base and incorporates DLA Energy's capabilities.

d. Title 10, US Code, Section 153, prescribes that, subject to the authority, direction, and control of the President and the Secretary of Defense, the Chairman of the Joint Chiefs of Staff will be responsible for: (a) formulating policies for the joint training of the Armed Forces, and (b) formulating policies for coordinating the military education and training of members of the Armed Forces. While logistics remains a Service responsibility, there are processes and tasks that must be considered when developing a CONOPS in order to optimize joint logistic outcomes. Joint bulk petroleum training is offered in order to allow logisticians to become exposed to and proficient in joint bulk petroleum operations. The Joint Petroleum Training Module and the Joint Petroleum Module Desk Guide are Web-based, self-paced educational programs for joint logistics staff officers who are responsible for managing joint theater-level petroleum logistics operations. Additionally, joint publications (JPs) may be found on the Joint Doctrine Education and Training Electronic Information System Web site.

5. Bulk Petroleum in the Joint Logistics Environment

a. The complex nature of the joint logistics environment (JLE) will determine how bulk petroleum support is delivered to the joint forces. Sustained logistics readiness in the JLE depends on a collaborative network of relationships throughout the operational environment and at all levels of command. The geographic combatant commanders (GCCs) have the primary function of planning, executing, and controlling bulk petroleum support in their areas of responsibility (AORs), across strategic, operational, and tactical levels.

b. At the strategic level, the combination of Service, agency, and commercial organizations constitutes the backbone of joint bulk petroleum logistics, which aid in the projection and long-term sustainment of the CCDR's joint bulk petroleum requirements. The strategic level emphasis is on utilizing the nation's industrial base to enhance the CCDR's capabilities through leveraging of strategic resources while maintaining flexibility in the face of a dynamic JLE.

c. At the operational level, the joint bulk petroleum logistician integrates strategic and tactical capabilities of the joint forces to meet the CCMD's operational requirements. The joint bulk petroleum logistician encounters the greatest challenges at this level because of the difficulty in integrating the capabilities from many providers who must project, distribute, and sustain bulk petroleum for the JFC.

d. Global providers (the Services, commercial partners, US Joint Forces Command [USJFCOM], US Transportation Command [USTRANSCOM], and CSAs, including DLA) are a critical component at this level. USJFCOM, working with its components, ensures the necessary force structure (personnel and equipment) for organizing, training, and equipping bulk petroleum support forces at the operational level. Department of Defense Directive (DODD) 4140.25, *DOD Management Policy for Energy Commodities and Related Services,* directs the substance of Service-specific bulk petroleum support. The Navy provides seaward and over-water bulk petroleum support to the high-water mark; the Army provides overland distribution of bulk petroleum support, including inland waterways; and the Air Force distributes bulk petroleum by air.

e. At the tactical level, the responsibility to install and operate tactical petroleum storage and distribution systems usually lies with the Services. The Services derive their sustainment primarily from the strategic and operational levels for bulk petroleum operations and leverage the benefits of that sustainment to permit freedom of action. The joint bulk petroleum logistician contributes to joint force readiness by applying the three imperative capabilities critical to success: unity of effort, JLE-wide visibility, and rapid and precise response. The ability to deliver sustained readiness can be viewed in the context of the integrating functions of planning, executing, and controlling within the JLE. The framework for bulk petroleum support within the JLE is characterized by Figure I-2.

f. JP 3-28, *Civil Support*, discusses the role of DOD capabilities used for homeland defense or disaster scenario. The JP 4-0 series of publications for logistic support applies in civil support. However, logistic planners consider both military and civil requirements and capabilities concurrently to avoid duplication of effort and valuable resources. Implementation and execution of logistic functions remain the responsibility of the Services and the Service component commanders. Each Service is responsible for the logistic support of its own forces, except when logistic support is otherwise provided for by agreements with national agencies, allies, or another Service.

Figure I-2. Joint Logistics Environment Operating Framework for Bulk Petroleum

CHAPTER II
CORE JOINT BULK PETROLEUM LOGISTICS CAPABILITIES

"The pipeline constructed to support Operation IRAQI FREEDOM is the longest operational IPDS [inland petroleum distribution system] tactical fuel pipeline the Army has ever constructed. It is longer and moved more fuel than any previous IPDS pipeline. To construct it, more than 1,300 twenty-foot ISO [International Organization for Standardization] containers were transported and more than 1,500 soldiers were required to build and operate it."

To Support Operation IRAQI FREEDOM, *Pipeline & Gas Journal,* **January 2004**

1. Introduction

a. Theater bulk petroleum operations revolve around a push-pull supply system. Land-based customers request fuel from the Army component's TSC, another Service component organization, or an agency assigned as the lead Service for bulk petroleum support. The TSC normally includes a petroleum section and a distribution management center. The petroleum section is tasked to manage and account for theater bulk petroleum. It also coordinates tactical petroleum operations and quality surveillance (QS) of bulk petroleum in the theater. The distribution management center schedules movement of product forward into the support area based on a combination of available storage, distribution assets, and anticipated customer demands.

Note: In smaller scale operations, Army-led Service bulk petroleum support may come from tactical-level units, such as a sustainment brigade rather than a TSC.

b. Bulk petroleum support for maritime forces is similar to that discussed above; however, sea-based customers interact more directly with terminal operators at DFSPs.

c. The basic stockage concept in theater operations is to have sufficient storage to support the most demanding OPLAN, and keep fuel on-hand inventories at or near maximum authorized levels, while using available transportation assets as efficiently as possible. During peacetime operations, this stockage concept may be modified by actual day-to-day needs, economic resupply concepts, threat conditions, and storage objectives. When demand exceeds availability, the JPO devises an allocation system to support the campaign plan or OPLANs approved by the CCDR.

d. DODD 4140.25, *DOD Management Policy for Energy Commodities and Related Services,* provides the overarching policy and responsibilities. DODD 5101.8, *DOD Executive Agent (EA) for Bulk Petroleum,* assigns DLA as the EA for bulk petroleum with the authority to re-delegate to DLA Energy. As outlined in DLA Memorandum to DLA Energy (dated 1 November 2004), DLA Energy is DLA's designated EA to carry out DLA responsibilities outlined in DODD 5101.8, *DOD Executive Agent (EA) for Bulk Petroleum.*

2. Bulk Petroleum Supply and Distribution Operations

a. Effective and efficient supply operations enable the projection and sustainment of joint bulk petroleum in the theater. It is the pillar upon which all the operational levels depend. Effective, efficient, and sustained joint bulk petroleum support is achieved by integrating Service, agency, and other capabilities. DLA Energy supports this goal by exercising strategic-level management responsibilities for consolidation and review of requirements, procurement, funding, budgeting, storage, and designated distribution of bulk petroleum to meet the operational requirements. DLA Energy exercises responsibilities for the ownership of bulk petroleum in non-tactical bulk storage through sustainment, restoration, and modernization (S/RM) funding for Service bulk petroleum storage and distribution facilities. S/RM is the facility asset program designed to sustain, restore, and modernize fuel facilities for the warfighter.

b. Political and military leaders conduct operations in complex, interconnected, and increasingly global operational environments characterized by uncertainty and surprise. Multiple simultaneous operations are also conducted rapidly across joint operations areas (JOAs) within a single theater or across boundaries of more than one GCC and can involve a large variety of military forces and multinational and other government agencies (OGAs). The JLE exists within this operational environment and consists of the conditions, circumstances, and influences that affect the employment of logistic capabilities. It also exists at the strategic, operational, and tactical levels of war; and includes the full range of logistic capabilities, stakeholders, and end-to-end processes.

c. Joint logistics spans the strategic, operational, and tactical levels of war. It is, however, at the tactical level where the principal outcome—sustained logistic readiness—of joint logistics must be measured. At the strategic level, joint logistics is characterized by the vast capacity of the Nation's industrial base, both government and commercial. At the operational level, joint logistics has its most significant impact. It is at this level that strategic and tactical capabilities, processes, and requirements intersect, and it is here where the essence of joint logistics resides. The tactical level represents that part of the operational environment where outcomes are realized and logistic support is Service-oriented and executed.

d. Many organizations have, or are currently developing, common operational pictures (COPs) for situational awareness. They can provide an effective tool for decisionmaking at all levels of the organization. Figure II-1 shows a graphical and textual description of the information exchanged among and between operational nodes involved in a notional bulk petroleum COP. The graphical description depicts the operational elements, organizations, and units that are required to exchange information directly with each other and the types of information they exchange. This figure also identifies the need to exchange information from one operational node to another. However, it does not show the connectivity between them.

e. The notional bulk petroleum COP information node diagram displays the strategic, operational, and tactical sources of bulk petroleum information; the sources of non-bulk petroleum information, such as geographic and weather data; and the flow of each type of

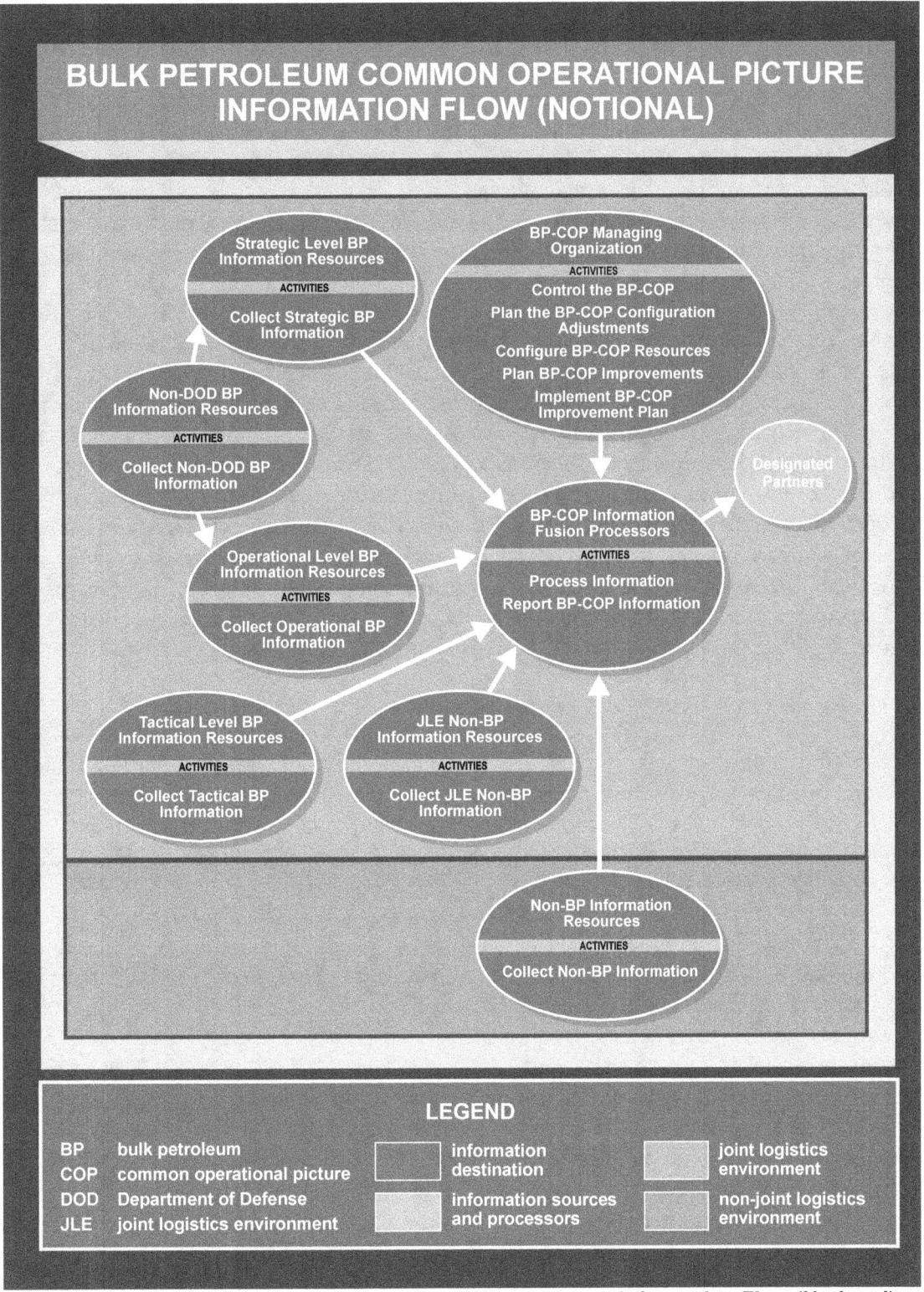

Figure II-1. Bulk Petroleum Common Operational Picture Information Flow (Notional)

information to the bulk petroleum COP processing center. It also shows that the processed information is made available for subsequent distribution to approved stakeholders.

f. Today's world is highly dependent upon petroleum products. Therefore, it is likely that some infrastructure would be available for use by US forces almost anywhere in the world. However, it is entirely likely, depending on the size of the operation, that sufficient in-place and operational fuel storage, on-hand product, road networks, rail lines, and easily traversed lines of communications (LOCs) would not exist to support planned operations. Therefore, tactical systems may be required to supplement infrastructure available in the theater.

g. Bulk petroleum may need to be received via joint logistics over-the-shore (JLOTS) operations. Such operations use an offshore petroleum discharge system (OPDS) or other bulk liquids transfer system to deliver fuel to tactical storage facilities located immediately ashore. The offshore system delivers fuel to a tactical or commercial terminal normally operated by a tactical pipeline and terminal operating unit. Fuel may then be moved forward through the use of trucks, rail, or installed pipeline systems that can quickly establish inland product distribution. If the theater is not an active theater of war, it should have an established peacetime operating stocks (POS) level and petroleum war reserve requirements (PWRR). The Army is generally tasked with the inland distribution of petroleum. The current Army doctrine is to provide support to joint forces using modular fuel distribution. Figure II-2 is an example of modular fuel distribution in the theater.

3. Web-Based Petroleum Contingency Report

a. The JPOs, at the direction of the Chairman of the Joint Chiefs of Staff, submit two key joint petroleum reports: bulk petroleum contingency report (REPOL) and bulk petroleum capabilities report (POLCAP). Information on frequency and how to complete these reports is outlined in Chairman of the Joint Chiefs of Staff Manual (CJCSM) 3150.14B, *Joint Reporting Structure—Logistics*.

b. The REPOL provides the Joint Staff, Services, and DLA Energy with summary information on bulk petroleum inventories, a damage assessment for bulk petroleum distribution systems, and other strategic information pertaining to bulk petroleum support posture at specific bases, posts, locations, and/or forward operating bases, etc. During contingencies, a REPOL can be submitted as frequently as daily or more often, as necessary. The JPO or SAPO consolidates the information to develop the REPOL for submission to the Joint Staff and supporting CCDRs using the Joint Chiefs of Staff (JCS) Web based REPOL application IAW logistics directorate of a joint staff (J-4) Memorandum, Subject: New JCS Web Based REPOL, dated 2 October 2008. The REPOL is widely used by the Service components, DLA Energy, JPO, and SAPO to manage theater resupply and distribution requirements and critical actions affecting theater petroleum distribution.

c. The POLCAP provides the Joint Staff, Services, and DLA Energy with an assessment of bulk petroleum support capabilities for contingency requirements in a specific theater.

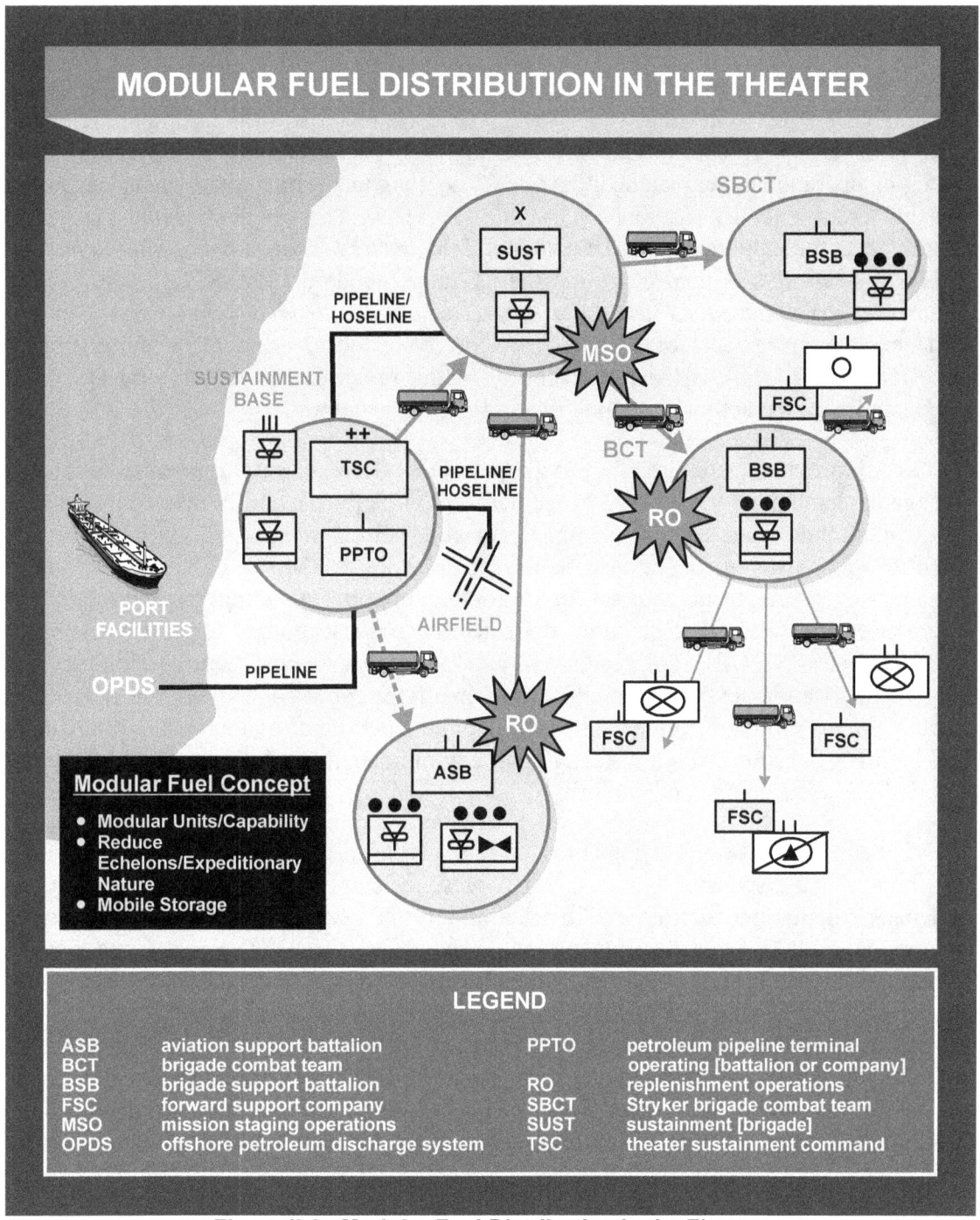

Figure II-2. Modular Fuel Distribution in the Theater

d. The JPO or SAPO develops a theater-unique version of the POLCAP and REPOL for their respective Service components and supporting DLA Energy regional office to use when reporting essential theater bulk petroleum information. They also publish the POLCAP and REPOL reporting instructions per their respective CCDR's logistic reporting directives.

4. Bulk Petroleum Quality Management

a. Quality management of bulk petroleum is essential to ensure bulk petroleum products are suitable for their intended use. The physical characteristics and complex chemical makeup of bulk petroleum products necessitates vigilance in quality management at the strategic, operational, and tactical levels. The two main functional areas of quality management are quality assurance (QA) and QS. Contract provisions detail the quality requirements for suppliers, while DOD 4140.25-M, *DOD Management of Bulk Petroleum Products, Natural Gas, and Coal* and the Military Standard (MIL-STD)-3004, *Quality Assurance/Surveillance for Fuels, Lubricants, and Related Products,* prescribe the quality management requirements for QA and QS performed by the government. With reference to these publications, QA is the responsibility of the procurement activity and QS is the responsibility of the activity handling the fuel until consumption.

b. All providers and users of bulk petroleum have a vested interest in quality management and must work closely together to provide the capability needed in this vital area of bulk petroleum support. Planning for bulk petroleum support, particularly those activities involving storage and distribution, must be designed around all available quality management assets from contract to customer support, including tactical petroleum laboratories and kits. That planning must also be fully accounted for in OPLANs and operation orders (OPORDs). Execution of bulk petroleum support requires a high level of diligence across all operations, including those involving captured petroleum stocks used by friendly forces in joint operations. The control of bulk petroleum quality management in the JLE involves the coordination of many civil, commercial, and military assets overlapping several lines of command and authority.

c. Sediment and water are the most common types of contaminants found in storage, distribution, and dispensing systems. Their presence can cause serious problems in fuel systems, particularly in aircraft. Positive action must be taken to prevent and eliminate the occurrence of these contaminants in bulk products. The DLA Energy and Service components must plan and ensure trained bulk petroleum quality personnel and equipment are available to ensure contingency petroleum stocks meet military requirements. QA ensures that suppliers have fulfilled their contract obligations and that the government is receiving the proper quantity and quality of specified bulk petroleum products. Petroleum QA is fulfilled when the product has been accepted by the government and becomes government-owned. Petroleum QS is an aggregate of measures applied to determine and maintain the quality of government-owned petroleum and related products so such products are suitable for their intended use. QS of bulk products begins upon receipt and continues as long as the products are in the physical possession of the government and until consumed. Responsibilities for QS:

(1) JPOs are responsible for establishing and maintaining a theater petroleum laboratory correlation program. They may subsequently designate either a Service or DLA Energy to manage and coordinate the correlation program. JPOs help ensure DLA Energy and components have a robust QS system.

(2) Services having physical possession of bulk petroleum are responsible for establishing and maintaining an adequate QS program. The Services shall also ensure that any instructions and procedures issued by them or under their authority conform to those agreed upon in MIL-STD-3004, *Quality Assurance/Surveillance for Fuels, Lubricants, and Related Products.*

(3) DLA Energy shall establish and maintain standardized quality management policy, programs, and procedures for DLA-owned products. DLA Energy furnishes direction and guidance in technical matters to all JPOs and quality personnel. All matters involving product quality will be coordinated with the technical offices of the Services prior to issuance. In addition, DLA Energy will initiate coordinated action to resolve any conflict of instructions and procedures between MIL-STD-3004, *Quality Assurance/Surveillance for Fuels, Lubricants, and Related Products,* and those issued by or under the authority of the Services.

(4) Personnel handling bulk petroleum products must be thoroughly trained and fully qualified to perform their assigned duties.

5. Fuel Safety

Safety is a principal concern. Petroleum products are hazardous due to their toxicity, explosiveness, flammability, and potential to create environmental damage. Prescribed safety precautions will be strictly followed for the protection of personnel, equipment, and the environment. Fire hazards are possible whenever petroleum products are handled, due to leaks, spills, vapor accumulation, improper grounding or bonding, or proximity of any heat source. Some of the key chemical properties of fuel and fuel additives that should be of interest to users are contained in MIL-STD-3004, *Quality Assurance/Surveillance for Fuels, Lubricants, and Related Products.*

6. Environmental Concerns

a. All US military activities are required to conform to US environmental laws and guidelines as set forth in DOD directives. Additionally, these activities must comply with all applicable state and local laws, rules, and ordinances, unless a waiver has been obtained from the appropriate authority, IAW Department of Defense Instruction (DODI) 4715.5-G, *Overseas Environmental Baseline Guidance Document.*

b. Leaks or spills must be avoided to prevent the discharge of petroleum products to waterways and underground water tables. Code of Federal Regulations, Title 40, Part 112.7, *General Requirements for Spill Prevention, Control, and Countermeasure Plans,* provides guidance on establishing a spill prevention and control plan.

c. Outside the United States, follow annex L of the relevant OPLAN and these environmental protection guidelines:

(1) Follow host nation (HN) environmental laws (when applicable), North Atlantic Treaty Organization (NATO) environmental standardization agreements, and regulations to the extent required by relevant status-of-forces agreements or other international agreements.

(2) Adhere to HN environmental requirements reflected in country-specific final governing standards (FGS).

(3) Where FGS are not in place, apply DODI 4715.05, *Overseas Environmental Baseline Guidance Document,* when HN environmental laws do not exist, are not applicable, or provide less protection to human health and the natural environment.

(4) Seek legal advice regarding the applicability of HN environmental laws or other US federal standards in contingency operations.

For additional information on environmental concerns, see DOD 4217.5, Management of Environmental Compliance at Overseas Installations, and DLA Energy Environmental Guide for Fuel Terminals.

7. Bulk Petroleum Operational Contracting Support and International Logistics Acquisition Agreements

a. Host-nation support (HNS) agreements, acquisition cross-servicing agreements (ACSAs), operational contracting support, and other agreements or treaties may include operational logistics acquisition authorities and are critical during contingencies when logistical support from US units for equipment may not be readily available, when forces have outpaced their internal logistic capabilities, or when acquisition of logistics support using these vehicles is more efficient or advantageous to the government. International agreements for acquisition and operational contracting support can be valid acquisition vehicles across all levels of military operations regardless of the size of the supported force, the complexity of the mission, or the location where operations occur. These acquisition instruments give the JFC a flexible and responsive way to support forces and their missions.

b. DLA Energy has responsibility for the centralized procurement of bulk petroleum for DOD. The contracting officer is the DLA Energy point of contact for questions and concerns regarding contract award or administration. For the Bulk Petroleum Business Unit, questions and concerns should be addressed to DLA Energy. The contracting officer may appoint a contracting officer representative (COR) to assist with administrative or quality issues. The scope and limits on the COR responsibilities are defined in the appointment documents.

c. DOD components must submit requests to GCC's JPO for validation and obtain DLA Energy authority to locally purchase petroleum products in excess of the annual limits described in DOD 4140.25-M, *DOD Management of Bulk Petroleum Products, Natural Gas, and Coal.* The contracting officers will respond with the information required in order to approve the request. However, in the case of bulk petroleum, requests should be submitted through the service control point (SCP) that will first validate the request and then forward it to the DLA Energy for approval. If a DOD component is not supported by a DLA Energy contracting officer, it should send all requests through the cognizant SCP or DLA Energy duty officer.

d. Into-plane contracts. DLA Energy into-plane contracts allow government aircraft from military and federal civilian agencies to purchase fuel and refueling services at commercial airports at substantial discounts from the posted airport price. The Services shall send requests for into-plane contracts through the CCMD JPO for validation to DLA Energy. However, the Services may use an Aviation Into-Plane Reimbursement Card without requesting DLA Energy authorization when the commercial airport lacks any DLA Energy into-plane contract coverage.

e. Emergency requirements. When requirements prohibit time to obtain a DLA Energy contract through normal procurement channels, the user determines the need for emergency procurement. Emergency procurement should cover only the amount calculated to sustain immediate operational needs and until normal contracting channels are secured. For work stoppages, local purchase is limited to immediate use quantity. Note: A copy of the local purchase procurement documents must be mailed to DLA Energy with the annotation: "Local purchase of a DLA-integrated managed item."

f. Contracting is commonly used to augment organic military and other sources of support such as multinational logistic support and HNS, but contracting is often not properly planned for or integrated into the overall JFC logistics support effort. Contracting support capabilities should be considered when needed to augment organic support capabilities and in situations where ACSAs or HNS agreements do not exist or when these agreements cannot provide sufficient bulk petroleum products. The supported GCC must ensure that there is a joint acquisition review board (JARB) or JARB-like process in place at the appropriate level (normally at the subunified command or JFC level) to determine the basic source of support and priority requirements. When support is contracted, the challenges associated with planning and executing that support include the following:

(1) Coordinating and executing the overall contracting effort IAW federal laws and regulations and ensuring adequate in-theater contract oversight and management.

(2) Centralized control and decentralized execution.

(a) Centralized control can be accomplished by mandating local procurement procedures through subordinate JFC contracting boards or through the designation of a lead Service or joint theater support contracting command.

(b) Decentralized execution is accomplished through the procurement authority vested in the contracting officer to exercise business judgment in the execution of the contracting mission. The Federal Acquisition Regulation (FAR), Defense Federal Acquisition Regulation Supplement, and local procurement policies may also mandate reviews of certain contractual actions prior to the contracting officer's signature.

(3) Coordination. The JFC is responsible for synchronizing and coordinating all contracting support actions in the operational area. This coordination prevents undue competition for the same limited commercial resources in the operational area; gives the JFC the ability to enforce priorities and control common logistic support efforts; and maximizes the utility of the limited contracting force supporting the JFC.

(4) Law and regulations. The GCC, subordinate JFCs, and their staffs must be cognizant that contracted support is planned for and executed IAW law and regulations. In

all military operations, contracting officers must award contracts IAW policies and procedures that implement legal requirements. Violating federal statutes and regulations pertaining to proper acquisition of goods and services can result in significant investigations, mandatory reporting to Service and DOD secretariats, and criminal prosecution.

(5) In-theater contract management. The GCC, subordinate JFCs, and supporting commanders must understand that contracting is not a "fire-and-forget" system. Contracting support to military operations requires significant planning and management efforts from both the contracting staff and the requiring activity. The JFC and component commanders must ensure that the requiring activities are properly trained and actively participate in the requirements generation and validation process. Requiring activities are typically obligated to provide personnel to be CORs. These personnel require formal or informal training to be ordering officials, field ordering officers (FOOs), government purchase card holders, or CORs. Ordering officials are trained and certified to make individual orders from blanket purchase agreements. FOOs are authorized to make small purchases for construction, supplies, and services using the Standard Form 44. The actual dollar limits for these items may change, but is generally limited to micro-purchase threshold amounts specified in the FAR. For service-type contracts, the JFC and component commanders must ensure that all supported units have sufficient certified COR personnel available to monitor contractor performance. Additional non-COR support, such as personnel to perform security checks or escort contractors, may also be required.

CHAPTER III
PLANNING FOR JOINT BULK PETROLEUM LOGISTICS

> *"By reducing the need for petroleum-based fuels, we can decrease the frequency of logistics convoys on the road, thereby reducing the danger to our Marines, Soldiers, and Sailors"*
>
> **Major General Richard Zilmer, US Marine Corps**
> **July 2006, Commander of US forces in the al-Anbar province in Iraq**

1. Introduction

The supported CCDR's JPO is responsible for the overall planning of petroleum logistic support for joint operations within the assigned AOR. This planning occurs at the strategic level and usually is embodied in the petroleum appendix to the logistics annex of the military OPLANs or CONPLANs. The petroleum appendix covers theater-wide fuel requirements, resupply, and distribution. The format for fuels planning is prescribed in CJCSM 3122.03, *Joint Operation Planning and Execution System (JOPES), Volume II: Planning Formats.* The DLA Energy regional offices and Service components support the JPO in developing a practical, sustainable petroleum support concept and plan.

For more information, see Appendix A, "Planning Guidance for Appendix 1 to Annex D, Bulk Petroleum Supply for Military Plans."

2. Joint Bulk Petroleum Operation Planning

a. Utilizing the joint operation planning process, logisticians responsible for supporting bulk petroleum within the JLE assemble an array of tools to assist with support planning for the projection, distribution, and sustainment of joint forces.

b. The LSA provides a broad assessment of key logistics capability areas required to execute the CCDR's plans. The LSA is a critical plan assessment tool that seeks to define the total unconstrained logistics requirement for the execution of a CONOPS. The LSA findings should highlight logistics deficiencies and their associated risks to supporting theater operations. Additional tools are the integrated consumable item support (ICIS) system, operation-logistic planners, and other planning documents.

c. Joint bulk petroleum plan development involves meticulous attention to the ability of global partners to provide bulk petroleum assets to the theater. The scope of this planning is widespread and involves the ability of contracting partners and HNs to complement the global partners' strategic capabilities. Plan development must also integrate the availability of secure LOCs, the intensity of current and future operations, and the organizational structure of the JFC. Whether through contingency or crisis action planning, the joint bulk petroleum planner must also have the capability to call upon the vast information resources available across all operational levels. The collection of data from disparate information systems is essential to garner accurate assumptions for contingency planning and substantiated facts for crisis action planning processes.

d. JFCs must be able to adapt to evolving mission requirements and operate effectively across a range of military operations (see Figure III-1). Some examples of the range of military operations include humanitarian assistance, disaster relief, and support to counterinsurgency. Joint petroleum logisticians must have a general understanding of the diversity, range, and scope of military operations and understand their role in each type of operation. They must develop mutually supportive relationships to enhance coordination between commercial companies, regional partners, and CCDRs. Petroleum logisticians must understand multinational and interagency petroleum capabilities and coordinate mutual support, integrating them into the joint operation, as appropriate. Many crisis response missions, such as foreign humanitarian assistance and disaster relief operations, require time-sensitive sourcing of bulk petroleum products and transportation for rapid delivery to the point of need. The primary challenges for petroleum logisticians during these types of operations are gaining visibility of the requirements, assessing competing priorities, and adjusting continuously as the situation unfolds to ensure sustained readiness over time.

e. A fundamental tenet to successful planning for bulk petroleum support is the early and accurate identification of requirements enhanced by the joint bulk petroleum planner's complete understanding of the commander's intent and CONOPS. This critical knowledge will enhance the ability to direct available bulk petroleum resources to

REQUIRED ACTIONS WHEN PLANNING FOR BULK PETROLEUM OPERATIONS

- Project accurate, timely fuel requirements

- Maximize use of in-country civilian or host nation support fuel facilities

- Tailor fuel equipment and support packages to the requirement

- Standardize and ensure compatibility of fuel equipment to support joint and multinational fuel operations

- Establish the theater joint petroleum office or subarea fuel manager with assistance provided by Defense Logistics Agency Energy regional offices and Service components

Figure III-1. Required Actions When Planning for Bulk Petroleum Operations

"Afghanistan's lack of road networks and infrastructure poses a serious challenge to the Marine Expeditionary Brigade's ability to receive and distribute fuel. All fuel used by NATO [North Atlantic Treaty Organization] forces in Afghanistan is brought in by tanker truck via Pakistan or from the countries bordering Afghanistan's north. Political frailties coupled with the lack of road networks and virtually nonexistent infrastructure creates bottlenecks and limits the ability to move large quantities, requiring constant monitoring and management. Additionally, the increased presence of contractors, multinational forces, etc., at a large number of forward operating bases not only increases the demand for fuel but also makes it impossible to maintain the 'single fuel on the battlefield' concept, further straining the system. This requires constant coordination with the contracting office and others to ensure contracts are written cognizant of these limitations and to require contractors to locally procure fuel or utilize equipment capable of utilizing JP-8 or an equivalent type of fuel."

Chief Warrant Officer-3 Ronald Groen, Bulk Liquids Officer,
Marine Expeditionary Brigade,
Afghanistan, Task Force Leatherneck

support the joint force and allow for greater flexibility in execution. The more integrated the logistics planning is with the development of the CONOPS and the commander's intent, the more effective the overall operational execution.

f. One critical aspect of joint bulk petroleum planning is the infrastructure where the operation will be conducted. Some theaters will have HN assets available, such as pipelines, storage facilities, and railways, that will help support the bulk petroleum distribution system. In these situations, airbases, tactical airfields, and other sites can be supported by pipelines whenever tactically feasible. In other theaters, HN or commercial bulk petroleum facilities may not be available and tactical assets will need to be used. Tactical bulk petroleum supply systems may include limited tanker mooring systems, floating hose lines, submarine pipelines, inland tank farms, temporary overland hose lines or pipelines, and collapsible tanks.

g. Within the planning process, the inventory management plan (IMP) is an important document that is validated and issued annually by DLA Energy in concert with the CCMDs and Services. The IMP identifies the petroleum inventory levels needed to support POS requirements and PWRR and specifies the amount of petroleum product, by location, held to cover requirements. These two categories of inventory guide the sizing of the stock levels to permit immediate and short-term operations across the range of military operations. Their purpose is to sustain such operations until resupply can occur.

h. To ensure an adequate supply of petroleum products in the initial phases of a contingency, the CCMDs and Services develop requirements to properly size petroleum war reserve stocks. The PWRR is based on the need to support specific joint operations until normal LOCs are established. The Joint Staff, in coordination with DLA Energy, develops guidelines, approved by the Office of the Secretary of Defense (OSD), on days of supply (DOS) and appropriate assumptions for secure sources of resupply. These guidelines are provided to the Services and CCMDs and serve as the basis for determining requirements. Using these guidelines, the Services develop and apply structured, auditable methods of computing PWRR for each OPLAN.

(1) PWRR for campaign plan or OPLAN. PWRR is the CCDR's war reserve fuel required to support a campaign or operation as outlined in the CCDR's campaign plan, OPLAN, or OPORD. The requirement is determined by applying operational tempo and fuel consumption rates to all the deployed weapon systems in the campaign or operation.

(2) ICIS is available to assist the joint logistics planner. ICIS develops PWRR by using the CCDR's time-phased force and deployment data (TPFDD) and applying Service consumption data in order to produce detailed time-phased requirements. ICIS output, coupled with Joint Flow and Analysis System for Transportation, is used to develop a sealift tanker delivery slate, in the form of non-unit TPFDD records. The ICIS force deployment module allows direct entry of forces into the module for crisis action and exercise planning when a TPFDD is not available.

i. The pre-positioned war reserve stocks (PWRS) are the on-hand products designated to satisfy the PWRR. They consist of stocks to support deployment and combat operations and are sized to meet requirements until resupply can be affected from a secure source. Sourcing assumptions and PWRS DOS factors are developed by the Chairman of the Joint Chiefs of Staff and forwarded to the Under Secretary of Defense for Acquisition, Technology, and Logistics (USD[AT&L]) for review.

(1) Establishment. PWRS shall be based on the most demanding operational plan requirement for each location and is in addition to POS for each location. The CCDR's JPOs are authorized to release or reallocate PWRS in emergency situations.

(2) Types of PWRS:

(a) Starter stocks are war reserve material located in or near a theater of operations to support the conduct of military operations until resupply at wartime rates can be established or the contingency ends, whichever occurs sooner.

(b) Swing stocks are positioned afloat or ashore and are capable of supporting the requirements of more than one contingency in more than one theater of operations.

j. The GCCs, with recommendations from the responsible Service component, prescribe the location, level of protection, and security of PWRS.

k. Petroleum POS are the amount of product required to sustain peacetime operations in support of military demands. The fuel POS levels are computed annually by DLA Energy for all DFSPs and utilize the factors depicted in Figure III-2.

l. Inventory management plan. A worldwide IMP is developed and issued annually by DLA Energy in coordination with the Services and CCDRs. The IMP identifies the

FACTORS FOR COMPUTING PEACETIME OPERATING STOCKS

Daily Demand Rate – The past and projected years' issues are used to calculate a daily demand rate.

Economic Resupply Quantity – The fuel quantity a defense fuel support point can receive that ideally balances economic and operational requirements.

Safety Level – The safety level is the amount of fuel to compensate for variability in resupply time and demand during the resupply cycle.

Unobtainable Inventory – That fuel needed to prime a storage dispensing system such as pipeline fill, manifold fill, and tank bottom below the suction line.

Figure III-2. Factors for Computing Peacetime Operating Stocks

required inventory levels, both POS and PWRR, and the amount of fuel by location stocked to cover those requirements. Because of storage limitations, one CCDR may cover the requirements of another CCDR's OPLANs with concurrence of the supported CCDR's JPO. Although not desirable, this practice is allowed when products can be delivered within the required joint OPLANs timeframe and before normal commercial resupply in a stockage location. To the extent practicable, and consistent with acceptable risk, stocks are positioned at or near the point of intended use. When possible, stocks are dispersed and held in conventional hardened facilities in high-threat areas. DLA plans for war reserve storage are coordinated with the CCMDs and fully consistent with HNS programs such as NATO's infrastructure programs, Combined Defense Improvement Project in Korea, and Japanese Facilities Improvement Program.

m. Joint bulk petroleum inventory. It consists of PWRS and POS. Both inventories are sized based on a concept of having enough fuel on hand until resupply can be assured. PWRS shall be in addition to POS and are designated as starter or swing stocks or both IAW DODI 3110.06, *War Reserve Materiel (WRM) Policy.* This approach optimizes stock levels to maintain an acceptable degree of support and sustainability across the range of military operations. Inventory levels are independently determined for each location or, where practical, for a defined area.

n. Emergency allocation of petroleum. Various levels of responsibility govern the allocation of fuel during a national emergency. These responsibilities are dependent on the theater and worldwide commercial environment. Based upon the CCDR's guidance, the JPO will direct the allocation of petroleum products. This allocation will include using PWRS to meet peacetime operations. Actions taken will be coordinated with DLA Energy. DLA Energy is responsible for providing the CCDR with the needed information on the overall fuel situation and efforts under way to overcome deficiencies.

o. If the Services or the CCMDs are not satisfied with the allocation of products by DLA Energy during constrained fuel availability, they may request the activation of the Joint Materiel Priorities and Allocation Board (JMPAB). The JMPAB, which acts for the Chairman of the Joint Chiefs of Staff in all petroleum allocation matters, will be established only under extreme situations where there are worldwide fuel shortages that will result in ultimate supply failure or in unacceptable degradation of wartime sustainability. Specific information that the Service or CCMDs must provide to the JMPAB includes current inventories, resupply forecasts, and impacts on both peacetime and wartime operations.

p. The prudent use of war gaming and exercises, either through simulation or other means, can be an important aid to identify gaps and clarify roles and responsibilities in bulk petroleum operational plans before they become problematic in execution. Modeling new concepts is a useful way to develop solutions without actual hostilities; however, the planner must be cognizant of depending too heavily on assumptions that would lead to inherently flawed conclusions.

q. Land forces. Primary fuel support for all theaters should be accomplished using the standard NATO approved fuel, whether a kerosene-based fuel or an alternative/renewable fuel, as approved by DLA Energy. Fuel support for ground equipment may be accomplished using commercially available diesel fuel when supplying kerosene-based fuel or an alternative/renewable fuel is not practicable, cost-effective, or required for commercial power generation equipment.

r. Maritime forces. Primary fuel support for maritime aircraft shall be the standard NATO approved fuel, whether a kerosene-based fuel or an alternative/renewable fuel with a high flash point. Conventionally powered ships should use a high flash point distillate-fuel. Military Sealift Command (MSC) ships and leased commercial ships may use commercial marine fuel for propulsion.

s. Overall theater petroleum support. The inland petroleum distribution plan (IPDP) provides a single source document for understanding how the guidance provided in the OPLANs or OPORDs will be executed. It provides the details necessary for Service commanders to understand how to interface with units, agencies, and firms providing petroleum support. Military weapon systems and equipment, including contractor-provided distribution and life support equipment, must be capable of using alternative fuels.

t. Just as the JPO is responsible for theater petroleum planning, the SAPO is responsible for bulk petroleum planning and execution matters within its operational area. This level of planning focuses on support for each Service component. Its products are the IPDP and base support plans. The IPDP complements the intratheater and intertheater planning efforts of the JPO and forms the tactical basis of the petroleum portion of the OPLANs and CONPLANs. The IPDP is published either as an annex to the petroleum appendix of the joint OPLANs or as a stand-alone document.

3. Bulk Petroleum Plan Development

a. The mission and the planned size and composition of the joint forces to be supported should be guiding parameters for planning efforts. Theater contingency scenarios, worldwide materiel distribution policies, and other guidance should be considered in determining specific theater requirements. CCDRs shall develop plans to minimize the types of fuels required in joint operations.

b. The following questions will aid in the development of the bulk petroleum appendix to annex D (Logistics):

(1) Should a SAPO for resupplying bulk petroleum be established?

(2) What is the CONOPS for petroleum support?

(3) What HNS is available?

(4) What are the components' responsibilities for petroleum support? Have components provided estimates of their bulk petroleum requirements?

(5) Have arrangements been made to contract for HNS or theater support contractor resources with the supported CCMD JPO or DLA Energy?

(6) Have bulk petroleum storage methods and sites been selected? What is the threat level within the operational environment? Have security arrangements for the sites been established?

(7) Have arrangements been made for transportation of bulk petroleum within the assigned theater?

Appendix A, "Planning Guidance for Appendix 1 to Annex D, Bulk Petroleum Supply for Military Plans," *provides additional planning guidance.*

4. Joint Bulk Petroleum Logistics Planning Considerations

The petroleum supply system must be designed for the operations and climate of the specific theater. Plans should consider at least the following points (see Figure III-3):

a. Mission. The mission and the planned size and composition of the joint forces to be supported should be guiding parameters for planning efforts. Theater contingency

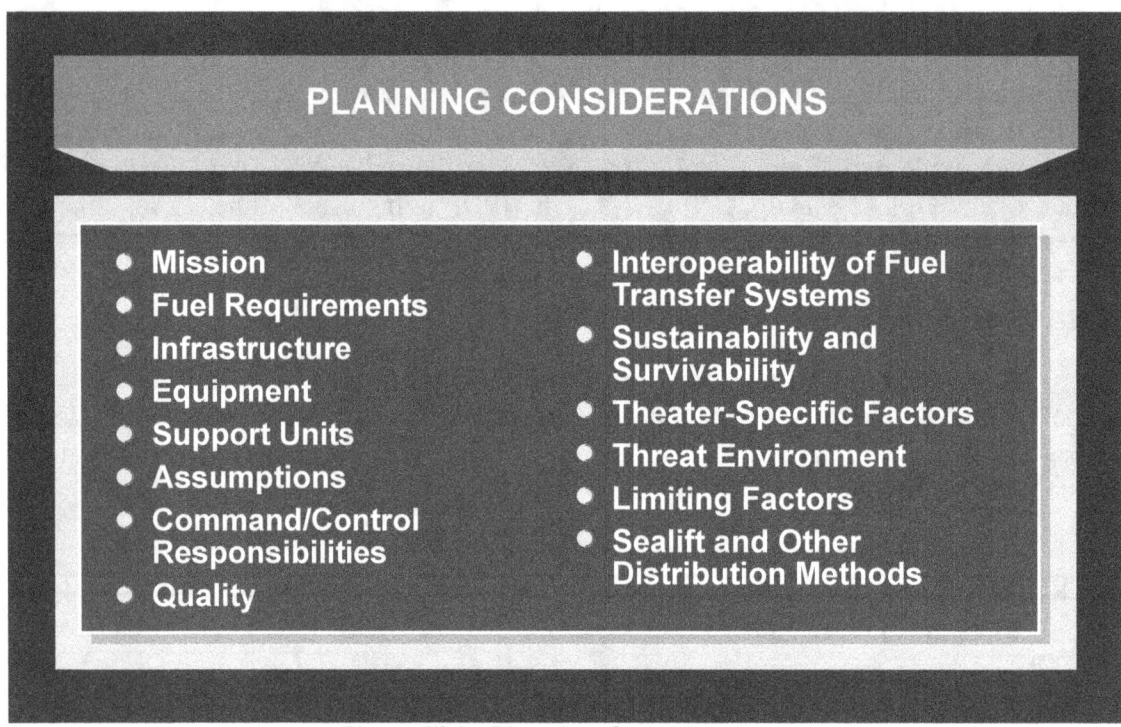

PLANNING CONSIDERATIONS

- Mission
- Fuel Requirements
- Infrastructure
- Equipment
- Support Units
- Assumptions
- Command/Control Responsibilities
- Quality

- Interoperability of Fuel Transfer Systems
- Sustainability and Survivability
- Theater-Specific Factors
- Threat Environment
- Limiting Factors
- Sealift and Other Distribution Methods

Figure III-3. Planning Considerations

scenarios, worldwide materiel distribution policies, and other guidance should be considered in determining specific theater requirements.

b. Fuel requirements. Fuel requirements to support the deployment and employment of forces are determined by the Services. Service components of the CCMDs (or other organizations within each Service) use such factors as troop strength; numbers and types of aircraft, vehicles, or ships; deployment times; and intensity and duration of engagement to determine time-phased petroleum requirements. Plans should include these Service-generated requirements, all pre-positioned stocks, and sources for resupply. Accurate fuel requirement forecasting is critical to supporting the warfighter's mission. Service headquarters (HQ) must ensure bulk petroleum requirement planners receive the necessary training and resources to accomplish this task. The IMP, developed annually by DLA Energy in coordination with the Services and CCMDs, details worldwide bulk PWRR and storage availability by location. The PWRR are sized based on resupply sourcing assumptions included in the DOS factors, which are developed by the Joint Staff and approved by OSD.

c. Infrastructure. The capability of installations and facilities in the operational area to provide fuel, storage, distribution, and laboratories must be considered. Size, capability, and maintenance status of offshore unloading facilities, terminals, distribution points, and bases are important to the logistic feasibility of the fuel plan. Collecting this information can help determine the need for and method of employment of tactical terminals, pipelines, hose lines, and other fuel handling equipment.

"The task force found that in DOD [Department of Defense] combat simulation exercises, each military service emphasized mission execution while adequate fuel supplies were considered a constant. DSB [Defense Science Board] asserted that doing so left DOD unaware of the potential effects of fuel efficiency on combat operations and of the vulnerability of the fuel supply chain. Furthermore, with no model of efficient or inefficient fuel use, DOD could not analyze fuel related logistical requirements as part of the acquisition process."

Finding #4, Defense Science Board, February 2008

d. Equipment. To ensure that petroleum handling and distribution equipment is available for support of operations, fuel deployment packages, and operational project stocks should be identified and considered for use. The Air Force fuels operational readiness capability equipment (FORCE) and the Army inland petroleum distribution system (IPDS) are examples of such equipment. In addition, each Service's operating units for the specific petroleum handling systems should be linked to those systems and identified for movement in the plan.

e. Support units. Identifying the type and arrival dates of units not tied to any specific equipment system and needed for various support roles is critical to any operational success. Timely arrival of engineer units (or logistics civilian augmentation program contractors) for construction of petroleum facilities and underwater construction teams for OPDS setup are some of the diverse types of support units that must be identified.

f. Assumptions. All assumptions used in development of the plan must be detailed. This requirement is necessary to determine the realism and expectations during review of the plan as well as in actual execution.

g. Command and control responsibilities. Identifying the roles of the various elements involved in a petroleum support plan are key. Establishing the relationships of the various elements to ensure their seamless integration and focus on delivering results is essential for successful planning.

h. Interoperability of fuel transfer systems. Interoperability should be considered and resolved in the planning process for at least the following interfaces:

(1) Tanker or oiler to Navy receiving ship, US Coast Guard receiving ship, seaport load and off-load facilities, and JLOTS systems.

(2) Airbase fuel storage and dispensing systems to receive fuel from commercial or military sources and issue fuel to Service component and multinational aircraft.

(3) Shore distribution systems to tactical fuel systems and equipment; such as IPDS, amphibious assault fuel system, and fuel tanker vehicles.

(4) No system or set of systems should be planned to be utilized together without proper interoperability validation through the appropriate SCP.

i. Sustainability and survivability. Both of these concepts should be factored into the plan to ensure petroleum logistic feasibility. Assumptions should be critically reviewed. Where appropriate, security requirements beyond general user security must be identified.

j. Theater-specific factors. Consideration must be given to theater-specific factors, such as available commercial and HN supply sources and transportation assets. Many of these sources of petroleum supply will have political, technical, and economic factors that limit their availability. These commercial and HN limiting factors must be taken into account when developing the plan to support the deployment, employment, sustainment, and redeployment of forces. Some factors that commanders and planners must take into account include the following:

(1) Force protection for contractor personnel, fuel equipment, and stocks.

(2) Contractor limitations with regard to support.

(3) Contractor required logistic support.

k. Threat environment. The JPO integrates and applies threat assessments and force protection measures in petroleum planning and operations. While theater-specific factors may require force protection actions for contractor personnel, petroleum equipment, and stocks, QA actions should also be considered. Ensuring adequate security may include specific countermeasures against tampering, adulteration, substitution, contamination, and other actions that could make the fuel unusable or potentially damaging to the end user.

l. Limiting factors. Most plans should have some limiting factors, such as lack of sufficient bulk petroleum storage in theater, inadequate transportation assets to close the supply chain, inexperienced force structure, or nonexistence of commercial petroleum infrastructure in the operational area. Any of these can quickly bring an operation to a halt and must be explicitly identified in the planning documents.

m. Sealift and other distribution methods. Every plan should identify and rationalize the distribution methods necessary to successfully conduct the plan as constructed, including the identification of the sealift, airlift, and overland transport of bulk petroleum in support of the plan.

n. Quality. Fuel quality problems can have serious consequences on DOD's mission. Poor quality fuel can degrade weapons systems performance and damage critical weapons components. Avoiding such problems is the responsibility of DOD fuel managers. An active and well-documented quality program and procedures are the best methods to ensure appropriate fuel is available to the warfighter.

CHAPTER IV
EXECUTING BULK PETROLEUM LOGISTICS

"[Fuel, replacements, spare parts, etc.]…must be asked for in time by the front line, and the need for them must be anticipated in the rear."

General George S. Patton, US Army
***War as I Knew It*, 1947**

1. Introduction

a. The transition from planning to execution can occur abruptly, in phases, or even concurrently. Execution begins upon receipt of an order. It is then that planning outputs become the inputs for execution. The goal of bulk petroleum support is to fulfill the requirements of the CCDR's CONOPS and intent.

b. Operations within the JLE framework will differ significantly and the joint bulk petroleum logistician must tailor execution accordingly. Peacetime execution relies heavily on available global partners and HNS structure. Crises response and limited contingency operations require the integration of military and nonmilitary governmental agency resources, mostly characterized by short, intense periods of bulk petroleum support. Civil support operations occur when the resources and capabilities of local, state, and federal agencies are outstripped by the requirements of disaster response. DOD organizations engage in immediate response or respond to requests for assistance from a lead federal agency.

c. The framework for bulk petroleum support calls for a joint staff organization with clearly defined roles and responsibilities for both the organic joint staff and the augmented component that provides specialized support. The use of various automated tools is essential to realize situational awareness, battle rhythm, assessment, and synchronization of bulk petroleum resources in the execution of an operation.

d. DOD bulk petroleum inventories consist of PWRS and POS. These inventories exist to support logistic requirements and are sized to cover a range of military operations. They take into account economic resupply, safety levels, unobtainable inventory, and deliberate planning requirements. As such, they are created to provide optimal peacetime and contingency support.

e. Two key joint bulk petroleum reports within the JLE are the REPOL and POLCAP. The details of these reports are described in Chapter II, "Core Joint Bulk Petroleum Logistics Capabilities."

f. During execution, the bulk petroleum logistician must track key metrics developed in the planning phase and reviewed in the execution phase. One source of these key metrics is the commander's critical information requirements. It provides the bulk petroleum logistician with the critical data the commander uses to measure success. Other sources of key metrics are friendly forces after-action reports; intelligence assessments; unit availability reports; intransit asset visibility; and HN and contracting partner capability reports.

g. As the execution phase continues to mature and eventually conclude, all or portions of the operation will cease and forces and equipment will be reallocated or even moved out of the theater. It is important for the bulk petroleum logistician to maintain awareness of these operations to support their proper conclusion and to assist in the reallocation of bulk petroleum resources.

2. Bulk Petroleum Logistics Execution

a. The established infrastructure within a theater supports the supply and distribution of bulk petroleum. Stocks are moved from secure military or commercial sources to forward areas and terminals as demand or plans require. The movement and redistribution of assets are accomplished through a joint effort involving the CCMDs, Service components, and DLA Energy, interfacing with USTRANSCOM components for product movement outside the operational area. In the early stages, the theater infrastructure may consist only of a minimal amount of HN commercial or military infrastructure supplemented by assets of a Marine air-ground task force or Army support area. Land-based customers request fuel from the Army component TSC, or another Service component organization or agency assigned as the lead Service for bulk petroleum support. The TSC normally includes a petroleum section and a distribution management center. The petroleum section is tasked to manage and account for theater bulk petroleum. It also coordinates tactical petroleum operations and QS of bulk petroleum in the theater. These organizations schedule movement of product forward into the corps support area based on a combination of available storage, distribution assets, and anticipated customer demands. The communications zone, including tactical airbases, may never be formed depending on the duration and geographic expansion of the operation. In all theaters, direct support units may provide fuel on an area basis to some or all MNFs comprising a joint or MNF.

b. Actual procedures to accomplish the delivery of products to the end user depend on the sources of product and the conditions in the operational area. The theater normally has some HN assets available or theater support contracts (i.e., fuel sources, terminal facilities, pipelines, railways, and trucks) that should be used to the maximum extent possible to help

---

LOGISTICS OPERATIONS CENTER

"The morning of the 16th [August 1990] began with our briefing by General Pagonis. Each person, based on his background, was given a subject area in which to work. I took the petroleum, water, and other general supply and maintenance functions....We calculated requirements on a day-to-day basis. This allowed other activities to take our basic calculations and organize them to meet their particular information needs. Since the fuel required for war would be vastly greater than for peacetime, we provided two fuel projections covering both of those alternatives."

Colonel John J. Carr, Starting From Scratch in Saudi Arabia, *Army Logistician*,
January–February 1993

---

offset US requirements. Because the capabilities of allies or coalition partners are theater unique, the JPO or SAPO is responsible for assessing these potential capabilities and integrating them into appropriate plans and operations. Figure IV-1 depicts normal land petroleum operations.

(1) Pipeline distribution. Pipelines are often the most economical and effective method of inland fuel distribution. Bulk petroleum is generally most efficiently moved from base terminals and rear storage locations to the combat zone by pipelines. A fully developed theater fuel distribution system may include ship discharge ports (with moorings and piping manifolds), seaside and inland fuel storage tanks, pump stations, and pipelines. Pipelines can be either the installed type or the tactical coupled pipeline version. The rapidly installed type is normally used for the initial phases of the operation and the more permanent coupled pipe for later phases. Large-scale operations may justify the construction of coupled pipelines using the Army's IPDS to move bulk petroleum forward from rear area storage locations, as illustrated in Figure IV-2. These lines may supplement existing Service or HN infrastructure pipelines. Airbases, intermediate support bases, and operational locations deemed appropriate may also be serviced by pipeline systems when tactically feasible. Pipelines can be very economical and effective when existing infrastructure is available; however, the decision to deploy a tactical system must first be tempered with the availability of resources to accomplish proper execution and sustainment. Tactical pipeline systems require extensive commitment of resources for engineering, transportation, and security support that may be unavailable or better employed elsewhere. Hose lines may be used to service smaller or temporary, large-volume sites. These tactical transfer systems can quickly establish inland distribution of bulk petroleum. The pipeline system extends as far forward as possible, with hose line extensions into sustainment brigade storage sites. However, the tactical plan should be considered before committing to extensive use of pipelines.

(2) Truck distribution. In many cases, truck distribution may offer the tactical commander more flexibility in the distribution of fuel. This distribution may be accomplished through use of military controlled or commercial assets.

(3) Tactical systems. A tactical tank farm consisting of collapsible tanks is constructed at airbases or other locations and connected to the main hose line or pipeline. The airbases or other locations then employ tactical servicing systems that have hoses, pumps, and filters to issue the product to the end user. These tactical issuing locations must also have the capability to test the fuel to ensure quality is maintained. In a theater, in-place and operational tankage, on-hand product, road networks, rail lines, and easily traversed LOCs normally are not available. Bulk petroleum may need to be received via JLOTS operations to deliver fuel to tactical storage facilities located immediately ashore. The OPDS delivers fuel to a tactical or commercial terminal normally operated by a tactical pipeline and terminal operating unit, as reflected in Figure IV-3.

(4) Air delivery. When LOCs are not secure or when operating in noncontiguous areas, Service component aircraft carrying fuel trucks, collapsible tanks, 500-gallon collapsible drums, or 55-gallon drums may be required to distribute fuel. Currently, aerial bulk fuel delivery system (ABFDS) enables cargo aircraft to transport from 3,000 to 30,000 gallons of fuel to the tactical storage and issue systems. Delivery amounts vary based on

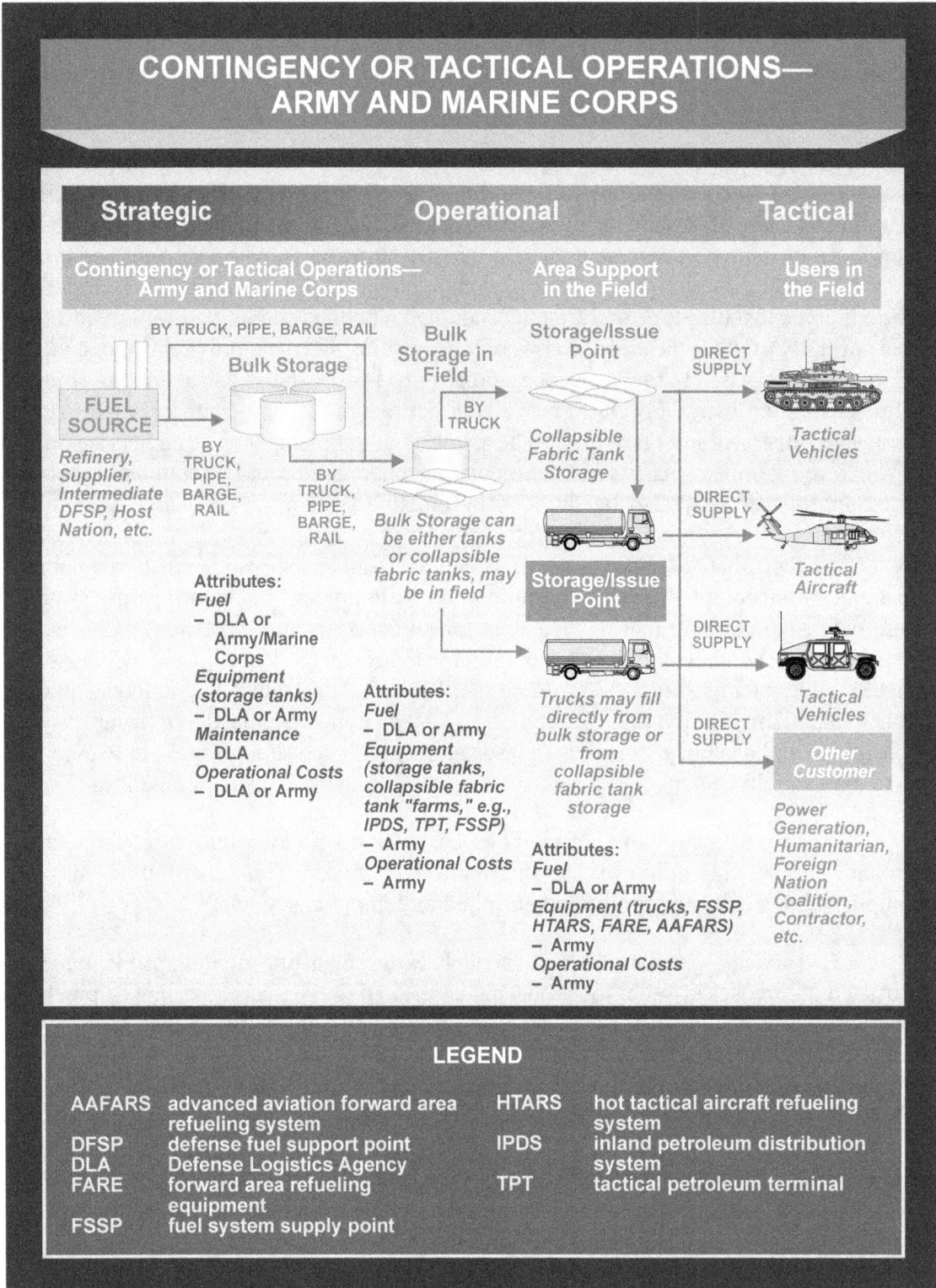

Figure IV-1. Contingency or Tactical Operations—Army and Marine Corps

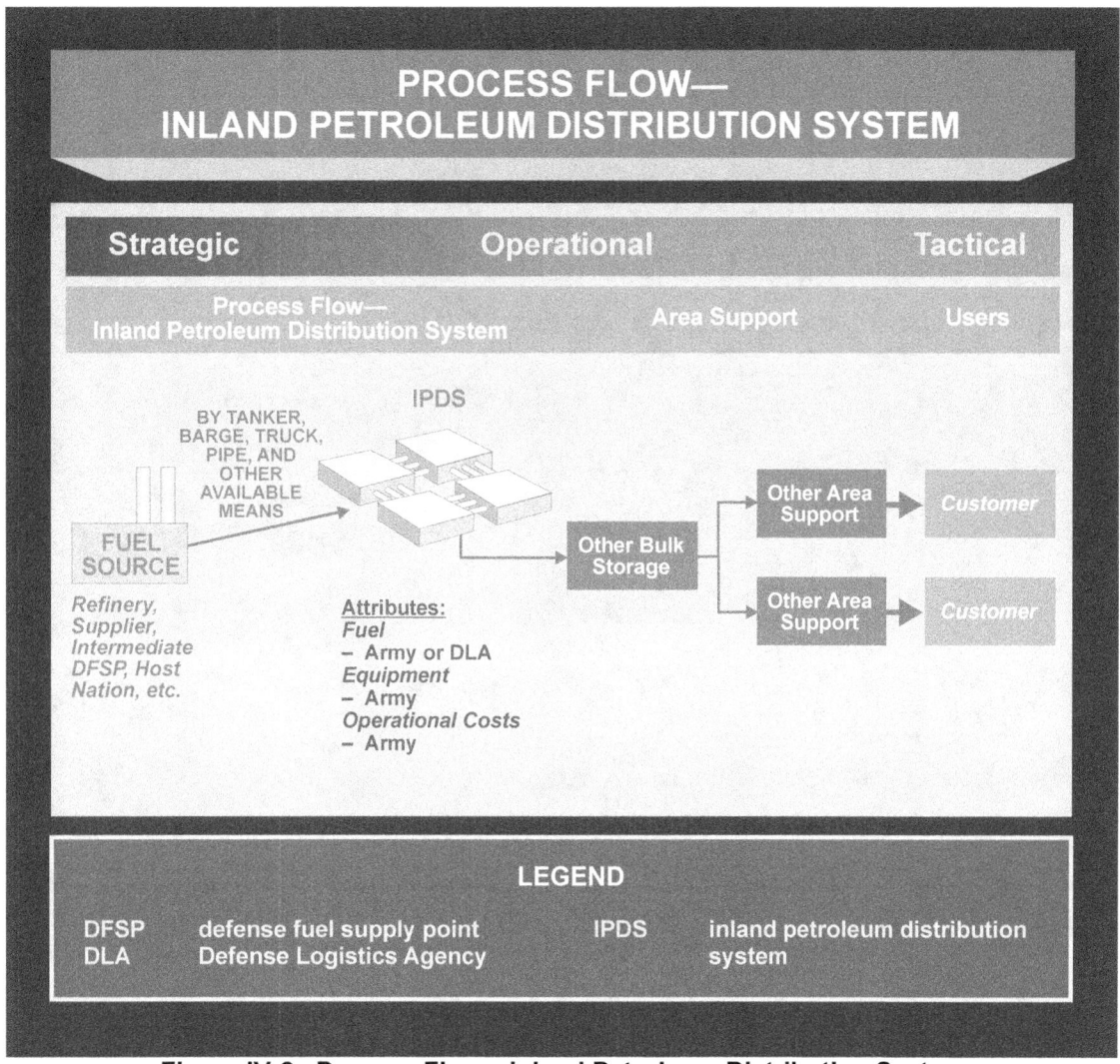

Figure IV-2. Process Flow—Inland Petroleum Distribution System

aircraft type, configuration, and runway capability. The tactical fuel distribution systems are typically air transportable and consist of collapsible tanks, hoses, filters, and pumps. The supply chain utilizing ABFDS is depicted in Figure IV-4. In addition, tanker and cargo aircraft can deliver fuel to airbase tactical systems, again depending on runway capability and the threat. Wet-wing defueling is transferring fuel from fixed-wing aircraft fuel tanks to collapsible fabric tanks or tank semitrailers. This method of bulk petroleum resupply allows the aircraft to carry an internal load of dry cargo plus aviation turbine fuel without requiring additional aircraft to provide fuel support. Wet-wing defueling can supplement other bulk petroleum delivery systems. Aircraft used in these defueling operations include the C-5, C-130, C-17, KC10, and KC-135. Transporting fuel by air greatly limits the airlift available for other requirements and is only used when other delivery means cannot meet operational needs. Transporting fuel by air also greatly increases cost as well as safety risks.

(5) Other distribution. The pipeline system may be supplemented by other means of bulk delivery, such as barges, rail tank cars, aircraft, bulk truck transports, and commercial distribution equipment provided by the host. These distribution systems are used to move

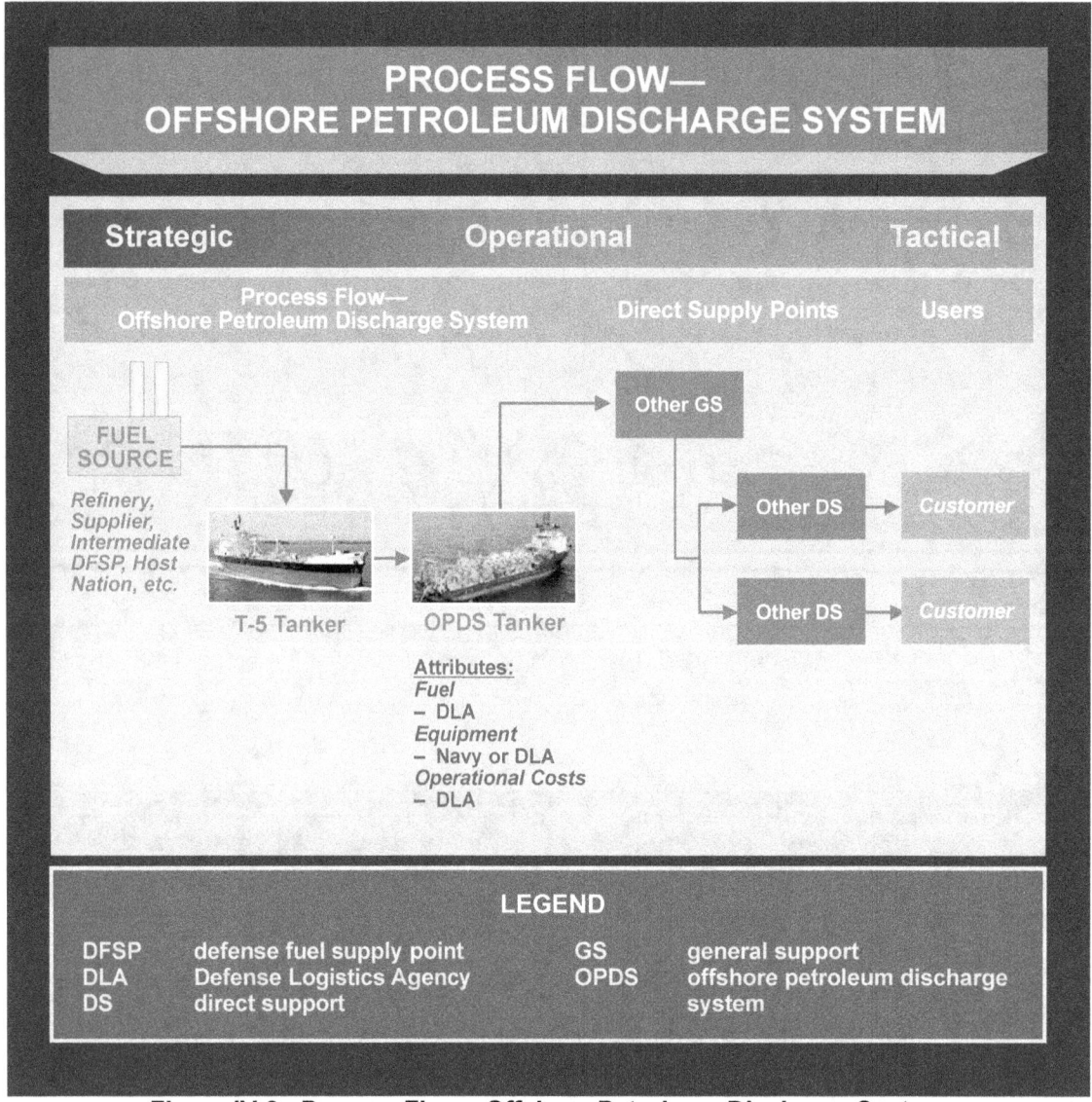

Figure IV-3. Process Flow—Offshore Petroleum Discharge System

products from the rear or intermediate areas to the multi-Service direct support echelons. Bulk truck transports commonly move fuel from terminals or corps area storage to the Service component direct support unit (i.e., petroleum support companies for the Army, bulk petroleum companies for the Marine Corps, base fuels flights for the Air Force, and construction force units for the Navy). Some local distribution is also made by tank trucks that are organic to these direct support units.

(6) Expanding distribution. As theater requirements expand, IPDS tactical pipelines, tanks, and fixed pumping assemblies may be installed depending on the volume of requirements, the expected duration of the employment, and the type of operation (e.g., foreign humanitarian assistance or peacekeeping). Other delivery means, operated either by military or commercial sources, such as tank trucks, barges, and aircraft, may be

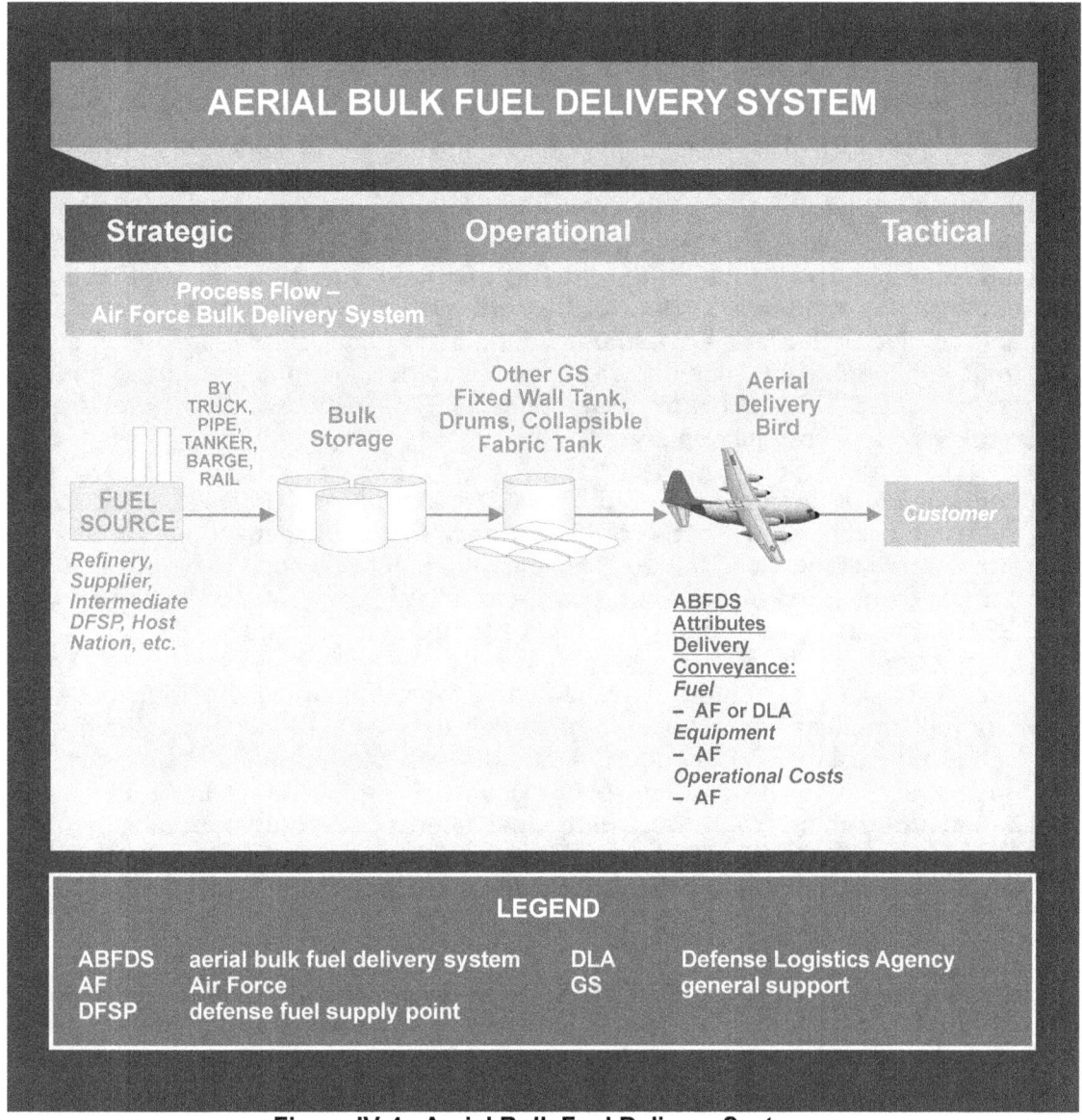

Figure IV-4. Aerial Bulk Fuel Delivery System

incorporated into the overall distribution system depending on road, river, or airport infrastructure.

(7) Airfield operations. Fuels support equipment required for initial support of airfield operations will be determined based upon fuel support requirements, real estate availability, HNS, method of resupply, etc. Initial support of airfield operations using refueling trucks may be sufficient at some locations. However, during Operation ENDURING FREEDOM and Operation IRAQI FREEDOM, the Air Force quickly realized the Vietnam era air transportable hydrant refueling system was not capable of efficiently supporting rapidly expanding aviation fuel requirements at most airfields. In order to address this situation, it deployed new FORCE, which includes the use of larger diameter hoses, higher capacity pumps and filters, additive injection capability, and programmable

---

**OPERATION IRAQI FREEDOM (OIF) SUPPORT—
TACTICAL PETROLEUM TERMINALS**

In addition to preparing subordinate units for war, the battalion's (240th QM [quartermaster]) most significant pre-war mission was to work with the 62nd EN BN [engineer battalion] to construct inland petroleum distribution system (IPDS) terminals and assemble pipeline to the Iraq border. However, the petroleum pipeline and terminal operating companies, with the doctrinal mission to operate the IPDS, did not arrive in Kuwait until well after construction had started. Without the right companies on the ground, every able-bodied Soldier, regardless of MOS [military occupational specialty] or their unit's doctrinal mission, was required to help manually emplace and construct 76 bulk fuel tank assemblies (BFTAs) in Kuwait to hold the required 11 million gallons of fuel.

Each BFTA is designed to hold up to 210,000 gallons; however, due to systemic problems, the bags could only be filled to 70% capacity to reduce stress and potential bag failure. This meant the battalion had to emplace 20 extra bags on the ground. After reconnoitering different sites with the 62nd EN BN, the plan was to build four tactical petroleum terminals.

Every unit and every Soldier was invaluable to the battalion in building these four fuel terminals in the three months prior to the war. Teamwork within the battalion was essential as subordinate units were task-organized to execute missions outside of doctrinal roles. Each unit had different capabilities, based upon their manpower, individual talents, or equipment that had arrived from the United States. Soldiers were cross-trained and with their equipment were cross-leveled, in order for the battalion to meet mission priorities, requirements, and timelines associated with building the IPDS infrastructure. The essential nature of teamwork and cross-leveling became an important and recurring theme throughout our mission and the "Proud to Serve" battalion adopted the unofficial motto and mantra of Whatever it Takes!

SOURCE: Colonel Shawn P. Walsh, US Army, Whatever It Takes: OIF
Theater Fuel Support in 2003, May 2007

---

logic control units to automatically meet changes in fuel flow and pressure requirements. Air Force/Base supply chain is depicted in Figure IV-5.

(8) Support units. Identifying the type and arrival dates of units not tied to any specific equipment system needed for various support roles is critical to any operational success. Timely arrival of engineer units (or logistics civilian augmentation program contractors or other contractors) for construction of petroleum facilities and underwater construction teams for OPDS setup are just some of the diverse types of support units that must be identified.

c. Interoperability of fuel transfer systems. Interoperability should be considered and resolved in the planning process for at least the following interfaces:

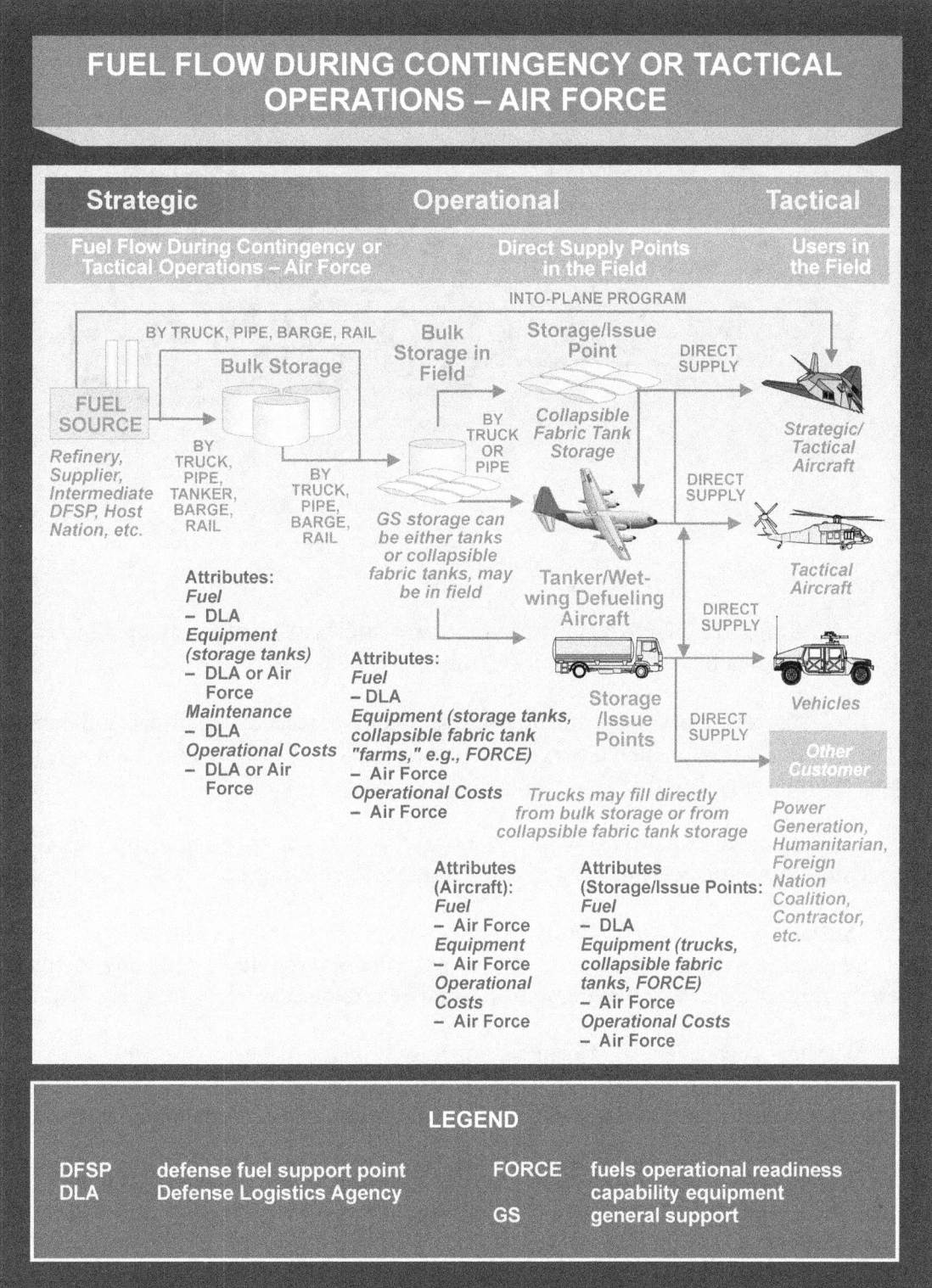

Figure IV-5. Fuel Flow During Contingency or Tactical Operations—Air Force

Tank trucks delivering fuel to forward locations.

(1) Tanker or oiler to Navy receiving ship, US Coast Guard receiving ship, seaport load and off-load facilities, and JLOTS systems.

(2) Airbase fuel storage and dispensing systems to receive fuel from commercial or military sources and issue fuel to Service component and multinational aircraft (e.g., fuels support equipment and ABFDS).

(3) Shore distribution systems to tactical fuel systems and equipment (e.g., IPDS, tactical airfield fuel dispensing system, and fuel tanker vehicles).

d. Sustainability and survivability. These concepts should always be factored into the plan to ensure petroleum logistic feasibility. Assumptions should be critically reviewed. Where appropriate, security requirements beyond general user security must be identified.

e. Theater-specific factors. Consideration must be given to theater-specific factors such as available commercial and HN supply sources and transportation assets. Many of these sources of petroleum supply will have political, technical, and economic factors that limit their availability. These commercial and HN limiting factors must be taken into account when developing the plan to support the deployment, employment, sustainment, and redeployment of forces. Some factors that commanders and planners must take into consideration include the following:

(1) Force protection for contractor personnel, fuel equipment, and stocks.

(2) Contractor limitations with regard to support.

(3) Contractor required logistic support.

Tactical storage in the theater of operations.

(4) Regional capabilities and intermediate staging bases to support strategic airlift transiting through the AOR.

(5) Regional capabilities to support Air Force tankers supporting air cap operations.

(6) Airfield limitations, maximum number of aircraft an airfield can have on the ground.

(7) LOC capabilities and limitations.

(8) Specialty fuel requirements.

f. Threat environment. While theater-specific factors may require force protection actions for contractor personnel, petroleum equipment, and stocks, QA actions should also be considered. Ensuring adequate security may include specific and appropriate countermeasures against tampering, adulteration, substitution, contamination, and other actions that could make the fuel unusable or potentially damaging to the end user.

3. Military Construction; Sustainment, Restoration, and Modernization; and Environmental Compliance

a. DLA, through DLA Energy, shall establish and maintain a DOD bulk petroleum distribution system and related programs in coordination with the Services and the CCMDs. DLA, Services, and CCMDs have interrelated responsibilities to plan and execute for military construction (MILCON), minor construction, operation of facilities, S/RM, and environmental compliance of bulk storage and distribution facilities in support of the bulk petroleum management mission.

b. The CCMDs assist DLA with the selection and prioritization of its fuel MILCON and qualified S/RM projects for petroleum facilities in their areas.

c. The Services assist DLA in the selection and assignment of a priority to the petroleum MILCON projects identified for the DLA MILCON program; they also provide technical support to identify and execute projects for DLA-funded S/RM and other qualified construction at the Services' petroleum facilities.

d. DLA reviews, analyzes, and validates the extent of the bulk petroleum storage and distribution facilities required in support of its bulk petroleum management mission in coordination with the Services and CCMDs through an annual program review. This program is designed to identify, fund, and execute bulk storage and distribution facilities projects in support of DOD petroleum objectives funded by DLA.

4. Bulk Petroleum Logistic Framework

> *"One final mission was conducted before transition of the bulk fuel mission to commercial contractors. The 110th had to store 3.7 million gallons of JP5 in two aboveground storage tanks. The unit worked around the clock, shuttling barges to and from the ship to refuel and download fuel into the tanks. Once this mission was completed, the unit began the transition phase of the operation."*
>
> **Captain Joseph W. Graham, 'Fuel Masters' in the Haiti Theater of Operations,**
> ***Quartermaster Professional Bulletin*, Spring 1995**

The CCMD logistic staff must be able to rapidly and effectively transition from peacetime or planning activities to monitoring, assessing, explaining, and directing logistic operations throughout the theater. As the operational tempo increases during a contingency or crisis, additional joint logisticians and selected subject matter experts (such as maintenance, fuel, and supply) can augment joint deployment and distribution operation centers by using established networks and command relationships instead of creating new staffs with inherent startup delays and inefficiencies.

5. Concluding Joint Bulk Petroleum Logistics Operations

Joint logistic operations are always ongoing, but it is possible that some logistics operations could be complete before the operation has been completed. For example, force reception operations could be completed when forces have moved to the tactical assembly area and been placed under the control of the commander for integration and employment, and no other forces are flowing into the operational area. It is important for joint logistics to monitor these transitional activities and ensure logistical resources used for the completed actions are given new tasks or the resources are redeployed back to home station. When operations are complete, joint logisticians should participate in the lessons learned process to review processes, roles, authorities, and the execution of the operation.

CHAPTER V
CONTROLLING JOINT BULK PETROLEUM LOGISTICS

"Unleash us from the tether of fuel."

General James T. Mattis, United States Marine Corps
During his 2003 tour as Commanding General
1st Marine Division in Operation IRAQI FREEDOM

1. Introduction

a. The ability of the joint bulk petroleum logistician to synchronize outcomes within the JLE presents serious challenges. Control of joint logistics requires organizing staff and operational level logisticians around their abilities to assist in planning and executing joint logistics support operations. It also involves integrating and synchronizing responsibilities, designating lead Service responsibilities, and developing procedures to optimize joint logistic outcomes.

b. Authority, responsibilities, and roles for bulk petroleum support involve many different commands. Service components and CSAs, must all work together in a single effort to ensure bulk petroleum support to the warfighter. Unity of command seldom shares the same place with the function of control within the joint bulk petroleum environment. The responsibilities to integrate, distribute, sustain, and synchronize forces and organizations do not diminish because of the lack of unity of command.

c. The JPO has the primary responsibility of synchronizing the diverse elements throughout the joint force. By designating a SAPO in the subordinate commanders' joint staff, the JPO enhances the ability to control outcomes that support the planning and execution of the operation.

d. Within the JLE, multinational and interagency operational arrangements become essential and permit US forces a freedom of action that may otherwise be unavailable. Within the context of controlling joint bulk petroleum logistics, serious consideration must be given to the diverse array of coalition and interagency petroleum logistics support structures.

e. The control of joint bulk petroleum logistics emphasizes unity of effort by integrating knowledge and experience with Service, multinational, agency, and other organizations' capabilities. This permits the logistician to exercise options, control organizations and staff elements, fuse information, and leverage technology. A scenario depicting some of the organizations, roles, and actions in planning for successful bulk petroleum support is presented in Appendix C, "Petroleum Scenario." The following sections describe in more detail the participants and roles in controlling bulk petroleum logistics.

2. Authorities, Responsibilities, and Roles

a. The integrated materiel management (IMM) concept underlies the principles in joint bulk petroleum doctrine. IMM is normally used when a single DOD agency has total management responsibility for supplying a specific product or group of related items to the Armed Forces of the United States. Because IMM both supports and influences this doctrine's usage and interpretation, an understanding of its conception is important.

b. The USD(AT&L) is responsible for establishing policies for management of bulk petroleum stocks and facilities, and providing guidance to other DOD agencies, Joint Staff, and Services. Additionally, USD(AT&L) is responsible for operating and maintaining area petroleum laboratories, where it has authority to test samples of petroleum products submitted for QA and QS, in coordination with the Military Departments. The Deputy Under Secretary of Defense for Logistics and Materiel Readiness serves as the central administrator for energy management and has IMM oversight responsibility for fuel products. The Under Secretary of Defense (Comptroller), in coordination with USD(AT&L), is responsible for establishing financial policies and guidance for management of bulk petroleum products.

c. The Chairman of the Joint Chiefs of Staff coordinates with DLA Energy, Services, and CCMDs to resolve petroleum issues. The J-4 is the primary agent of the Chairman of the Joint Chiefs of Staff for all bulk petroleum matters. Key responsibilities of the J-4 that influence joint petroleum principles and affect operations are listed below:

(1) Act as the focal point for joint bulk petroleum doctrine.

(2) Make recommendations to DOD on wartime fuel sourcing and pre-positioning DOS.

(3) Prescribe CCMD procedures for reporting bulk petroleum.

(4) Provide fuel inputs to the JSCP and review fuels planning in prescribed joint OPLANs.

3. Joint Petroleum Office and Subarea Petroleum Office

a. The GCC has the predominant fuels responsibility within a theater, and this responsibility is discharged by the JPO (see Figure V-1). The JPO works in conjunction with its Service components, SAPOs, and DLA Energy to plan, coordinate, and oversee all phases of bulk petroleum support for US forces and other organizations, as directed, and employed or planned for possible employment in the theater. JPOs typically have a mix of Service representatives. Operational requirements may dictate the establishment of SAPOs in support of subordinate JFCs. However, consideration should be given to the operational area and expected mission support, force composition, and sustainment requirements when selecting SAPOs.

KEY PETROLEUM RESPONSIBILITIES OF THE COMBATANT COMMANDERS WITH JOINT PETROLEUM OFFICES

- Plan and coordinate the receipt, storage, and distribution of petroleum products in theater in coordination with the Defense Logistics Agency (DLA) and Service component commanders
- Coordinate, validate, and prioritize petroleum military construction
- Provide petroleum logistic planning and policy guidance to component commanders
- Negotiate, in coordination with DLA, formal host nation support and coordinate the development and release of alliance or coalition petroleum planning information
- May assume temporary operational control of defense energy support center elements overseas in a major emergency in accordance with a coordinated memorandum of understanding
- Make maximum use of available stocks in adjacent theaters to support regional contingencies
- Direct tactical movement of fuels by means available to any Service component in a theater
- Plan and coordinate the use of captured or abandoned enemy bulk fuel assets
- Coordinate and negotiate multinational petroleum support
- Ensure fuel requirements, operations, restraints, and constraints are addressed in the fuels annex of operation plans
- Establish lead Service or agency responsibilities for Common Class III support as appropriate for each separate joint operation
- Release or reallocate theater war reserves in an emergency
- Validate Service component bulk fuel requirements in wartime or during contingency operations
- Decide, in coordination with DLA, between military and contract fuel support
- Integrate threat assessments and force protection measures into petroleum planning and operations
- Ensure components and DLA Energy have a robust quality surveillance program

Figure V-1. Key Petroleum Responsibilities of the Combatant Commanders with Joint Petroleum Offices

b. A SAPO is a sub-office of a JPO and is established by the CCDR or JFC (usually upon JPO recommendation) to fulfill bulk petroleum planning and execution matters in a section of the theater for which the JPO is responsible. A theater may have more than one SAPO. SAPOs are normally required to:

(1) Conform to the administrative and technical procedures established by the CCDR and DOD 4140.25-M, *DOD Management of Bulk Petroleum Products, Natural Gas, and Coal.*

(2) Be under the operational control of the JFC.

c. The key duties and responsibilities of the SAPO include the following:

(1) Advise the JFC and staff on petroleum logistic planning and policy, and provide Service components and commands with the JFC's petroleum logistic plans and policy.

(2) Prepare directives concerning the management, accountability, operation, and QA of petroleum activities in the operational area.

(3) Prepare petroleum input for JFC supporting plans and develop daily demand profiles and petroleum supply and distribution plans for OPLANs and OPORDs.

(4) Establish a direct LOC with the CCMD JPO concerning all aspects of petroleum activities.

(5) State bulk petroleum requirements through the CCMD JPO to DLA Energy to obtain sourcing from DOD stocks, local commercial, or host government resources using DLA Energy contractual coverage or service/country fuel agreements.

(6) Submit REPOL as required to the CCMD JPO.

(7) Assign JFC priorities and advise the CCMD JPO and DLA Energy for MILCON and S/RM projects for petroleum facilities.

(8) Validate existing quantity and quality of local inventories, estimated DOS on hand, and method and quantity of daily resupply capability by product.

(9) Coordinate and advise the CCMD JPO concerning local petroleum capabilities.

(10) Establish JFC requirements and coordinate with the JPO and DLA Energy for leased storage and related activities in the operational area.

(11) Coordinate with the HN and local commercial entities to determine availability of commodity and capability to support bulk petroleum operational requirements; identify or submit requirements IAW current HNS agreements to the HN for petroleum support.

(12) Supervise bulk petroleum operations; coordinate with commercial sources and host governments for the use of tanker loading and off-loading facilities.

(13) Coordinate with the DLA Energy, CCMD JPO, and Service component bulk petroleum managers to maintain visibility of bulk petroleum operations.

(14) Maintain operational petroleum delivery requirements from Service component petroleum managers to maintain visibility of bulk petroleum operations.

(15) Consolidate component delivery requirements and forward them to DLA Energy.

(16) Coordinate QS and procurement inspection programs.

(17) Advise the JFC, under emergency conditions, on the allocation of bulk petroleum and facilities, and coordinate with component control points.

(18) Release or reallocate PWRS.

(19) Notify the J-4 and CCMD JPO when PWRS will be penetrated and provide a plan for reconstitution of levels including a time frame when levels will be covered.

(20) Maintain thorough knowledge and understanding of JFC OPLANs and OPORDs, and component and supporting forces concepts of operations and support.

(21) Coordinate allocation and construction of inland petroleum distribution system assets.

(22) Provide broad guidance and supervision to the SAPO members.

(23) Track and account for all ground fuel movements in the area of operations to include deliveries to non-capitalized locations. The SAPO cannot complete this task unless a requirement for the SAPO to be notified of all completed deliveries and of any diversions while en route is established. In the absence of an established SAPO the reporting requirements would remain at the JPO.

4. Service Component Theater Bulk Petroleum Organizations

a. Each Service provides for product handling at its operational locations. The Services coordinate all fuel issues with the appropriate JPO, SAPO, and DLA Energy during single-Service, joint, and multinational operations, including exercises and deployments, to ensure efficiency and avoid duplication of effort. Normally the Army will provide distribution of bulk petroleum within theater. When required, and if the equipment assets are available, other Services may be tasked to supplement (or assume) the theater bulk petroleum distribution mission.

b. With increasing contractor support, Services must constantly review their responsibilities for tactical petroleum functions. In many cases, DLA Energy can have fuel delivered to the point of end use. But in some cases, such as extremely austere environments, delivery that far forward may not be possible. It is unlikely that contractors would be able to provide military performance specification (MILSPEC) fuels to an operational area during the earliest stages of an inland-based operation. Therefore, it is imperative that the Services participating in land-based operations (primarily Air Force and Army) have the capability to inject needed additives into commercial fuels until DLA Energy or Services can arrange delivery of MILSPEC fuels or contract support for additive injection, including equipment, training, and technical ability to inject additives. Further, joint and Service planners should know about these special requirements for additives.

c. Additives are a packaged product and usually ordered through Defense Supply Center Richmond. DLA Energy can assist and sometimes assume the responsibility for supplying additives needed to convert commercial products for customer use. Additionally, the Services need to forecast their needs for additives to DLA Energy regional HQ or DLA Energy HQ. These DLA Energy elements can order and arrange for transportation of the additives to as close to the point of intended use as possible. In the early stages of a tactical operation, the appropriate Service may end up transporting the required additives into the theater.

d. Inspection, sampling, testing, and documentation are required by each Service and agency to assure quality of fuel products received, stored, issued, and used. The applicable Service military specification custodians are responsible for development and maintenance of petroleum product specifications in support of aviation and ground fuels. To perform the petroleum support mission, each Service is responsible for the items shown in Figure V-2.

For additional information on QA and QS, see DOD 4140.25-M, DOD Management of Bulk Petroleum Products, Natural Gas, and Coal, *and MIL-STD-3004,* Quality Assurance/Surveillance for Fuels, Lubricants, and Related Products.

(1) Army. The Army normally provides management of overland petroleum support, including inland waterways, to US land-based forces of all DOD components. The Army provides the necessary force structure to install, operate, and protect tactical petroleum storage and distribution systems, including pipelines. In a theater, this responsibility also includes providing a system that transports bulk petroleum inland from the high-water mark of the designated ocean beach (IPDS/OPDS operations).

(2) Air Force. The Air Force shall maintain the capability to provide tactical support to Air Force units at improved and austere locations. It shall also provide distribution of bulk petroleum products by air where immediate support is needed at remote locations. The Air Force satisfies this requirement with the ABFDS for aerial bulk delivery and the ABFDS with alternate capability equipment for delivery directly to aviation assets. Additionally, the Air Force can accomplish forward area petroleum support through wet-wing refueling operations. At larger airfields, the Air Force shall provide the fuels support equipment to support expanding aircraft operations.

PETROLEUM RESPONSIBILITIES OF THE SERVICES

- Operate petroleum facilities under Service ownership
- Implement fuel standardization policies
- Assist Defense Logistics Agency (DLA) in selection and assignment priority of fuel military construction projects and provide base-level technical support for DLA funded maintenance, repair, and construction at its fuel facilities
- Manage Service-unique theater-assigned bulk petroleum transportation assets
- Compute wartime petroleum demands based upon combatant commander operation plans, wartime fuel consumption rates, war reserve requirements by location, and establish daily wartime demand profile
- Organize, train, equip fuel support forces
- Services requiring fuel additives should have or be able to obtain the necessary training and equipment to put additives into bulk fuel in austere environments
- Validate Service bulk fuel requirements

Figure V-2. Petroleum Responsibilities of the Services

(3) Navy. The Navy shall provide seaward and over-the-shore bulk petroleum products to the high-water mark for US sea- and land-based forces of all DOD components. It shall maintain the capability to provide bulk petroleum support to naval forces afloat and ashore (to include US Coast Guard forces assigned to DOD).

(4) Marine Corps. The Marine Corps shall maintain a capability to provide bulk petroleum support to Marine Corps units.

(5) Coast Guard. The Coast Guard shall coordinate petroleum requirements with the Navy.

5. **Managing the Joint Bulk Petroleum Supply Chain**

a. The Director, DLA, is responsible for meeting designated petroleum support requirements of the DOD components. These functional responsibilities have been delegated to the Director, DLA Energy, and include procurement, ownership, QA and QS, accountability, budgeting, and distribution of bulk petroleum stocks to the point-of-sale.

b. DLA Energy manages the bulk petroleum supply chain from source of supply to the point of customer acceptance as the DOD EA and IMM for bulk petroleum.

c. These responsibilities mandate that DLA Energy exercise total DOD-level management responsibility for bulk petroleum, including the requirements, funding, budgeting, storing, issuing, cataloging, standardizing, and procuring functions. The roles between the JPO, SAPO, Service components, and DLA Energy have become more integrated due to the ownership of DOD bulk petroleum and the expanded role of DLA Energy's support to the warfighter. Key functions of DLA Energy that influence joint bulk petroleum principles and affect operations include the following:

(1) Procure fuel to meet US military requirements in both peacetime and war, making every effort to purchase military specification fuels.

(2) Plan, program, budget, and fund facility maintenance and repair and construction of new fuel facilities.

(3) Administer and fund maintenance, repair, construction, and eligible environmental remediation projects in coordination with the Services and CCMDs.

(4) Plan, program, budget, and fund contract storage and associated services, to include refueling vehicles and equipment or aircraft servicing contracts, if appropriate, for bulk petroleum support.

(5) Negotiate and conclude international agreements in conjunction with the CCMDs to provide bulk petroleum support overseas.

(6) Develop contingency support plans in concert with supported commanders to acquire the necessary petroleum products, storage, and services.

(7) Provide technical support to the applicable military custodian responsible for development and management of petroleum product specifications.

(8) Allocate resources in support of PWRS, compute POS requirements, and develop an IMP that identifies inventory levels, storage, and covered requirements.

(9) Develop the annual quantity of bulk PWRS in coordination with the Services and CCDRs.

(10) Continuously evaluate the petroleum market and advise OSD, Joint Staff, and Services of resupply issues critical to peacetime and wartime operations and planning, such as adjusting DOS or recommending augmented safety levels for products and locations where the commercial market base cannot react to surges in demand.

(11) Acquire the necessary petroleum product, storage, and/or services within an AOR, to include non-tactical refueling vehicles, equipment, and refueling contracts, to support military requirements.

(12) Assure delivery of Class III bulk petroleum as close as possible to the point of intended use or to where it can reasonably be expected to be delivered by the contractor; address force protection issues to the supported CCDR.

(13) Assume management of wholesale bulk petroleum facilities that the CCMD JPO or SAPO has acquired for support of US forces in a mature theater.

(14) Contract, in consultation with the supported CCDR, for inland petroleum distribution as far forward as possible.

(15) Establish regional offices to facilitate practical and responsible decisions that ensure expeditious delivery of fuel products to each Service, DLA Energy established regional offices to maintain close contact with customers to ensure their particular needs are considered when planning fuel support. In general, DLA Energy regional offices coordinate delivery orders with industry, resolve logistic problems, supply emergency products, perform QS and management activities, coordinate maintenance and repair projects, and assist the JPO in petroleum logistics planning. During an emergency, DLA Energy may also place additional liaison officers at the appropriate command levels.

6. Commander, United States Transportation Command

a. The Commander, USTRANSCOM, shall plan for and provide air, land, and sea transportation of fuels for DOD during peacetime and wartime. These efforts will supplement and not replace the primary responsibilities assigned to the Services and DLA, especially with regard to intratheater and inland fuel movement and distribution. Other bulk petroleum responsibilities include developing long-range plans, in coordination with CCMD JPOs, for petroleum support of the intertheater mission and contingency operations worldwide, monitoring all en route MILCON projects, and overseeing and validating fuel data reporting and requirements by Air Mobility Command (AMC) and MSC to the CCDRs. The JPO, USTRANSCOM, represents Commander, USTRANSCOM, on all petroleum and water-related issues involving USTRANSCOM and components.

b. The key duties and responsibilities of the USTRANSCOM JPO include the following:

(1) Prepare plans, policies, and procedures for executing petroleum operations as they relate to supporting the USTRANSCOM strategic mission.

(2) Develop long-range sustainment plans for petroleum support of USTRANSCOM's intertheater mission and contingency operations worldwide.

(3) Review long-range plans for positioning of petroleum assets.

(4) Serve as a voting member on DLA's Installation Planning and Review Board, providing command recommendations on budgetary expenditure for out-year MILCON projects.

(5) Oversee and validate all fuel data reporting by AMC and MSC.

(6) Assist warfighting commanders on establishing their fuel-related priorities.

(7) Participate in all standing En Route Infrastructure Steering Committees, analyzing fuel-related issues.

(8) Coordinate with other JPOs to deconflict requirements.

7. Multinational Partners

a. General. CCMDs should make maximum use of HN and theater support contracted capabilities to meet peacetime and wartime requirements, particularly when logistic support from US units or equipment may not be readily available, when combat forces have outpaced integral logistics capability, or when acquisition of logistics support using these vehicles is more efficient or advantageous to the government. The type and amount of fuel support provided should, if possible, be specified in signed agreements and included in logistic plans of all nations concerned. The amount of support, civil or military, an HN can provide depends on its national laws, industrial capability, and willingness to give such support. Although sometimes difficult to obtain, HNS agreements should be aggressively pursued.

b. Agreements. Several different agreements, such as NATO standardized agreements, defense cooperation agreements, bilateral agreements, implementing arrangements, foreign-assistance acts, foreign military sales programs, and reimbursement for multinational support, may serve CCDRs' and Service components' needs, depending on the degree and type of support required and the specific HN.

c. Negotiations can occur with the HN under the auspices of an ACSA or a stand-alone international agreement. An ACSA is usually negotiated by the CCMD and is authorized under the acquisition and cross-servicing authorities, Title 10, United States Code, Sections 2341–2350. DLA Energy, as delegated by DOD through DLA, has overall responsibility for negotiating, concluding, and amending international agreements for petroleum support. A stand-alone international agreement is usually negotiated by DLA Energy or a Service through the appropriate US embassy as authorized in DODD 5530.3, *International Agreements*. That directive provides the basis for the following guidance except where superseded by law.

(1) Fuel exchange agreements are negotiated with foreign governments to provide fuel support in the international arena and to improve relations between the US and foreign militaries. In these agreements, products are supplied on a reciprocal basis, either with an exchange of fuel or cash payment, between the military organizations of both countries. These agreements are operational tools that enhance sustainability and readiness, because countries routinely train and support each other.

(2) Assistance in kind (AIK) operations, dealing directly with the governments of these eligible countries, provide materiel and services for a logistic exchange of materiel and services of equal value. These items are accountable as future reimbursements to the country that initially provides them on a gratis basis. Costs for these items have a current value that is captured as future reimbursements. The JFC comptroller will develop and implement procedures, in coordination with logistic elements, to track the value of support provided to

ensure an equal exchange of valued materiel and services throughout the operation. Particular care must be taken in accounting for these authorized exchanges due to the political sensitivity inherent in multinational operations. Ideally, AIK operations should derive no monetary gain and should provide mutual benefit and equity between the participating countries.

8. Contracts and Agreements

a. Blanket purchase agreement (BPA). A BPA should be considered for filling anticipated repetitive needs for supplies or services for a stated time period. Individual BPA purchases shall not exceed the simplified acquisition threshold, with the exception of commercial item purchases, which may be substantially larger. For current ceilings, see FAR Part 13.

b. Into-plane/into-truck contracts. Circumstances frequently require refueling military aircraft at commercial airports where military facilities or personnel are not available. To minimize commercial costs and ensure quality products will be available, an into-plane contract may be established. Once the supported CCDR defines the requirements, the contracts are negotiated by DLA Energy. An into-plane contract guarantees a quality product but does not guarantee a specific quantity of product. Any Service, CCDR, or federal agency may request that DLA Energy establish an into-plane contract. Noncontract fuel purchases may be made at civilian airports using the Aviation Into-Plane Reimbursement Card where DLA Energy has not established an into-plane contract. Into-truck contracts are similar to into-plane contracts but can be used to fill Service or contractor vehicles for distribution to customers not at the airfield. Services can establish off-site storage facilities to meet requirements around the clock and not tied to the operating hours of the airport. This type of contract takes advantage of the established commercial resupply capability to the airport while meeting non-aircraft requirements.

c. Bunker contracts. These contracts are similar to into-plane contracts and are used for frequent refueling of ships at commercial ports where DLA Energy has no DFSP. The requirements for bunker contracts are sent to DLA Energy for contract administration.

d. Direct delivery and post camp and station (PC&S) contracts and transportation tenders. DLA Energy, as the EA for worldwide petroleum support, can establish a variety of free on board origin and destination direct delivery PC&S contracts, and transportation tenders to support the CCDR.

e. HNs, through agreements, can provide a variety of environmental services, while the JFC is expected to comply to the maximum extent with local laws and regulations.

f. The use of wartime host-nation support (WHNS) bulk petroleum infrastructure and transportation assets in a mature theater is a critical part of the IPDP. The JPO or SAPO must ensure Service components are aware of potential WHNS infrastructures and that requests are forwarded and updated for joint OPLAN and requirements for contingencies are submitted in a timely manner. Each operational area and contingency will have unique procedures and policies for submission and approval of WHNS requests. It is the JPO or

SAPO responsibility to interface with CCDR WHNS agencies and ensure that all Service component requests are submitted and acted upon in a timely manner. During the adaptive or contingency planning process, a key element of friendly information the JPO or SAPO and Service component fuel planners must acquire is WHNS bulk petroleum infrastructure and distribution capabilities that potentially could be dedicated to support US forces. By leveraging the dedicated and trusted WHNS bulk petroleum infrastructure and distribution capabilities, the JPO or SAPO can dedicate the finite organic tactical bulk petroleum assets for those areas of the operational area that require tactical-level support. Fuel requirements for HNS can be provided to DLA Energy International Agreements Office for negotiation of an agreement with a foreign government to cover terms, conditions, and prices.

g. Fuel or storage support is also provided by commercial sources within foreign countries to US military forces. These types of contractual arrangements are routinely negotiated by DLA Energy to provide fuel support at international air or sea ports to meet military requirements.

9. Lead Nation

Under the lead nation (LN) concept, one nation agrees to assume responsibility for coordinating or providing a range of logistic support services to either all or part of an MNF. Such services may include transportation, medical support, medical evacuation, rear area security, port of departure operations, engineering, and movement control. Often, LN assignments are based upon geographic considerations. For example, a communications zone or operational area may be divided into sectors with LN responsibilities assigned to the major force in that area. Thus, more than one LN may service an operation based upon the division of geographic areas. Commanders designated by their nations to assume LN responsibilities must coordinate logistic support for forces within their geographically assigned limits. National contingents receiving LN support must maintain appropriate liaison with the LN.

INITIAL SUPPORT OF DEPLOYING FORCES

In January 2005, DESC [Defense Energy Support Center] had into-plane fueling contracts at 188 airports outside of the US. These contracts provided for fuel servicing in 103 foreign countries, and provided the foundation for fuel support for rapidly deploying forces. The annual contract quantities exceeded 284 million gallons of aviation fuel. These contracts provided the mechanism for rapid expansion of fuel support for contingency operations worldwide. Most of these airports do not provide JP-8. Only 22.3% of the contract quantity was for JP-8, while the vast majority of fuel (67.2%—over 190 million gallons) under contract was Jet A-1 without FSII [fuel system icing inhibitor] or CI/LI [corrosion inhibitor/lubricity improver]. Russian commercial fuel designated TS-1 made up 10.5% of the DESC into-plane contract quantities. Most commercial airports outside the United States do not offer Jet A-1 with FSII or CI/LI because the commercial airlines do not want these additives in the fuel they use. Both of these additives are surface active agents (surfactants) that can interfere with the ability of the filtration systems to remove water from jet fuel.

In addition to consuming over 190 million gallons of commercial Jet A-1 without FSII or CI/LI from into-plane contracts, CENTAF [Air Force US Central Command] activities issued over 106 million gallons of Jet A-1 without FSII or CI/LI to coalition aircraft during CY [calendar year] 2003. Most of this unadditized fuel was issued to airlift aircraft while locations primarily servicing fighter aircraft injected the additives into fuel during receipt into the bulk storage systems. Additives were injected to the maximum capability that additive, equipment, and personnel resources allowed. Nevertheless, almost 107 million gallons of Jet A-1 without FSII or CI/LI were issued, with the bulk of the unadditized fuel going to airlift aircraft.

SOURCE: *AFPET [Air Force Petroleum Office] Fuels Capability Study,*
Additive Deletion
Cost/Benefit Analysis, September 2005

Intentionally Blank

CHAPTER VI
PRINCIPLES OF BULK WATER PURIFICATION, STORAGE, AND DISTRIBUTION

"When the well is dry, we know the worth of water."

Benjamin Franklin, *Poor Richard's Almanac*, 1746

1. Introduction

a. **Water is one of the largest and most important life-sustainment commodities.** As water requirements rise above individual or small unit needs, they need to be handled in "bulk" form. Bulk handling calls for special equipment, product-handling safeguards, and standing operating procedures. Interestingly, bulk water is still foraged for on the modern battlefield.

b. **Commanders and their staffs at all levels must be concerned about maintaining water support to allow completion of the unit's mission. To provide the most effective use of water stocks and equipment, water planners must be familiar with Service, DOD agency, and CCDR water assets and responsibilities.** To ensure adequate support, commanders and their staffs should address planning for tactical water support in all plans and orders.

c. Water is supplied as either a packaged or bulk product. A packaged product is manufactured and procured, stored, transported, and supplied in a container. Water in larger quantities is a bulk commodity. Planners must consider alternative supply methods for bulk water. Packaged methods require extensive shipping, require materials handling equipment to move, and provide a reduced throughput capability when compared with bulk operations. Planners should weigh the advantages and disadvantages of packaged and bulk water carefully to ensure the best method is chosen to support the contingency.

2. Tactical Bulk Water Operations

Tactical bulk water support operations are implemented to purify water as close to the user as possible. This methodology involves detailed planning for the water point selection site and the purification, storage, and distribution of bulk water.

a. **Bulk water support responsibility.** Effective water support is essential to mission accomplishment. **Bulk water support normally is a Service responsibility.** However, during joint operations, if delegated authority by the GCC, the subordinate JFC may assign water support responsibilities on an area basis using the "lead-Service methodology," i.e., the dominant user or the most capable Service in an area may be tasked to provide water support to all forces operating in that area. The actual procedures used to provide bulk water support to the Services will depend on conditions in the operational area.

b. **Distribution. In most situations, water distribution is the "weak link" of the water support system.** Moving water from the production and storage sites to the user can be equipment and manpower intensive. Joint forces must make efficient use of all available assets in conducting water distribution operations. Transporting water from the storage site to the using units can involve utilizing various means from bottled water, water cans, the 2,000-gallon load handling system compatible water tank rack "Hippo," to the Marine Corps 45,000-gallon water distribution asset.

3. Planning Guidance

a. **Water planners at all levels must include water supply procedures and guidance in exercise and OPLANs.** Planners also need to ensure that the force has adequate resources for water purification, storage, and distribution.

b. **Water support planning is a continual process that begins with the identification of the force size and planned deployment rate.** Time-phased water requirements are then determined and units are selected and scheduled for deployment based on the requirements. Total water requirements are placed in the theater "water distribution plan" developed by the CCDR, with support from the Service component commander (see Figure VI-1).

For more information, see Appendix B, "Planning Guidance for Appendix 2 to Annex D, Water Purification and Distribution for Operation Plans."

c. **Planning for water support begins with determining water requirements.** Water requirements will depend upon the environment, the tactical situation, and the size of the

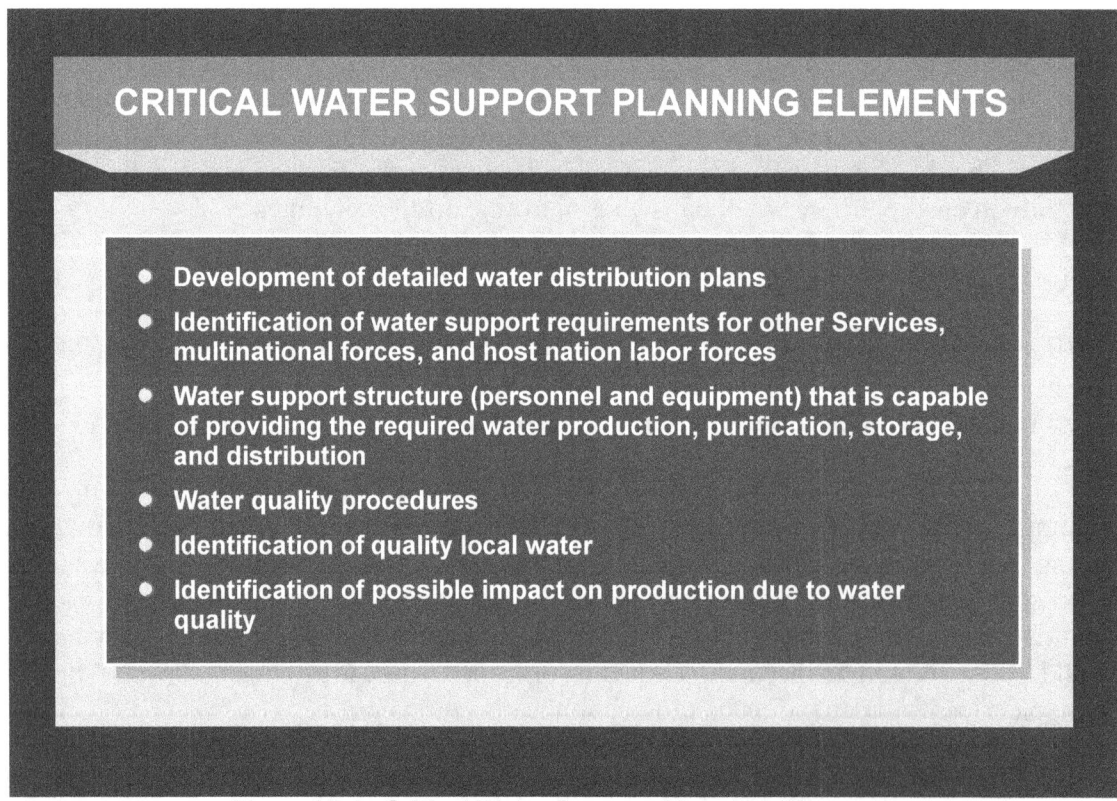

CRITICAL WATER SUPPORT PLANNING ELEMENTS

- Development of detailed water distribution plans
- Identification of water support requirements for other Services, multinational forces, and host nation labor forces
- Water support structure (personnel and equipment) that is capable of providing the required water production, purification, storage, and distribution
- Water quality procedures
- Identification of quality local water
- Identification of possible impact on production due to water quality

Figure VI-1. Critical Water Support Planning Elements

force. **Water requirements may vary daily.** Some requirements, such as cooking, may be indefinite while others may only be for a specific period of time.

4. Consumption Requirements

Water consumption requirements are based on the size of the force. Figure VI-2 lists the requirements and considerations.

a. **Region.** Water consumption also depends on the region. Water sources normally are abundant in temperate, arctic, and tropical regions. Although non-potable water is easily available, treatments may be required for certain or all uses. For this reason, non-potable water should be included in consumption estimates if treatment is necessary. In arid regions, water sources are sparse and water must be transported forward. In arid regions, in early phases of establishing base camps or forward operating bases, requirements for both potable and non-potable water will be met with potable water in order to prevent having two separate water systems. As a result, total potable requirements will increase in the arid regions. As operations mature, the focus should change to water conservation and reuse, and separate water systems should be planned for and established. In all regions, plan for 10 percent of the water to be lost through evaporation or waste.

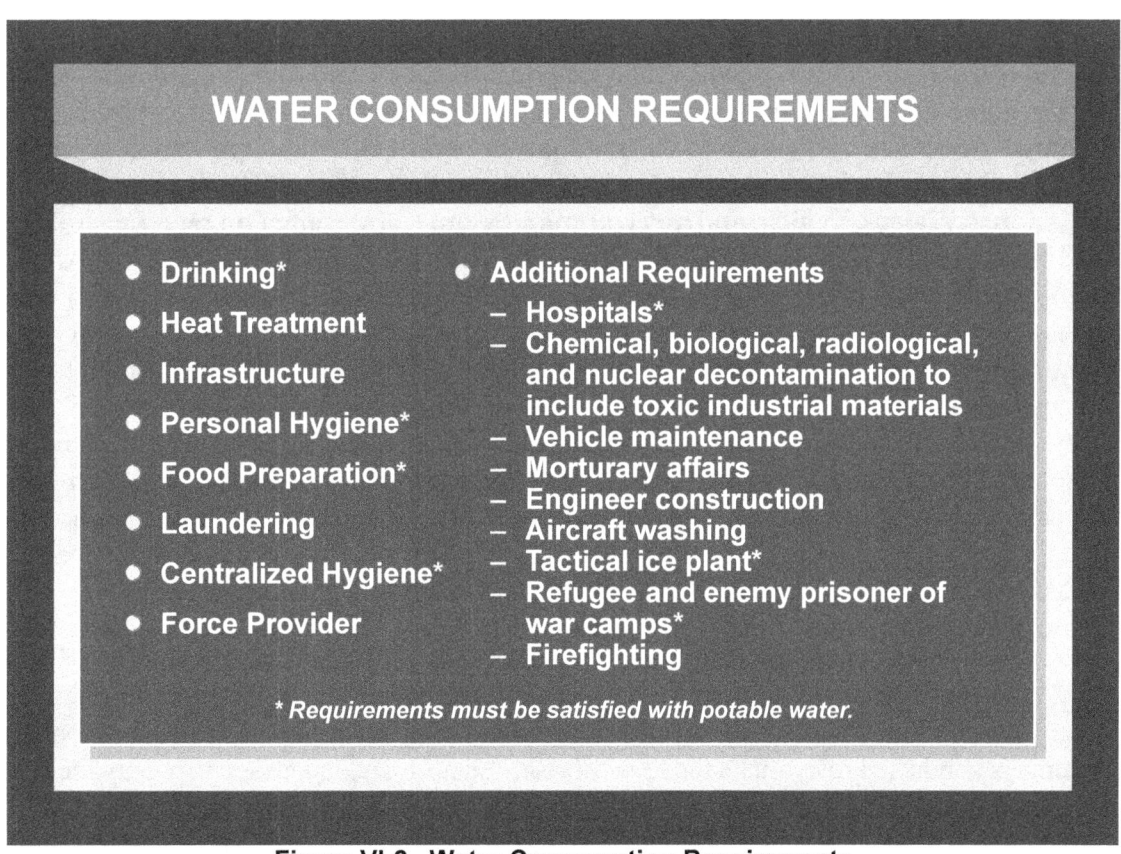

Figure VI-2. Water Consumption Requirements

b. **Requirements determination.** Several computations must be made to determine supply, purification, and storage requirements for water.

(1) **Supply requirement.** To compute the total daily water requirement of the force, multiply the actual strength by the proper consumption factor found in the Services' water consumption planning guides. The total, expressed as gallons per day, includes 10 percent for evaporation and waste loss.

(2) **Purification requirement.** To determine the amount of purification equipment needed to support the daily requirement, divide the total daily requirement by the daily production capability of one purification unit. Additionally, the type of water purification equipment selected will vary depending on the chemical makeup of the raw water. Under normal conditions, water purification equipment is operated 20 hours per day. However, many other factors affect water production.

(3) **Storage requirement.** Temperate, tropical, and arctic regions usually do not require large amounts of water to be stored. Raw water sources may be adequate to meet non-potable requirements, and the potable requirements can be met by the water purification unit's organic storage tanks. In arid regions, large quantities of potable water must be stored. The storage requirement is based on resupply times, daily requirements, and the DOS requirements established by the commander. In arctic regions, the storage of water may be complicated by freezing temperatures.

c. **Essential consumption.** When enough potable water cannot be produced to meet all the requirements, all but essential consumption must be reduced. **Essential water requirements include drinking, personal hygiene, field feeding, medical treatment, heat casualty treatment, personal contamination control, and patient/equipment decontamination in** chemical, biological, radiological, and nuclear (**CBRN) environments and, in arid regions, vehicle and aircraft maintenance.** Consumption rates under these conditions are classified as "minimum," enough for a force to survive up to one week. Requirements exceeding one week are classified as "sustaining." In this classification, nonessential consumption includes centralized hygiene, laundry, and construction. To optimize water treatment equipment, unit commanders may decide to use non-potable water for showering, laundry, and personal or patient decontamination after performing a risk assessment in cooperation with preventive medicine personnel. Preventive medicine personnel should screen for the presence of health hazards, such as skin-absorbed chemicals and pathogenic microorganisms. Non-potable water may require rudimentary treatment to be safe for these activities. Preventive medicine personnel should document troops' exposure to untreated water containing hazardous substances and organisms.

d. **Water vulnerability assessment.** Vulnerability of the water system to CBRN attack, conventional attack, and man-made/natural hazards must be considered. Normally, a water vulnerability assessment of potential and existing water sources and distribution systems is conducted to evaluate the level of risk. Ensuring adequate security may include specific and appropriate countermeasures against tampering, adulteration, substitution, contamination, and other actions that could make the water unusable or potentially damaging to the end user.

5. Water Support Operations

a. **Phase I, Water Purification.** Once an adequate water source has been identified and located, water purification is the first phase of tactical water support operations. During the purification phase, water is drawn from a source and purified to potable standards. Potable water is certified safe for human consumption. Water typically is purified with a reverse osmosis water purification unit. Standards are verified by medical service personnel responsible for water surveillance. The amphibious assault bulk water system is used to support Marine Corps amphibious assaults and maritime pre-positioning force (MPF) operations. It consists of 10,000 feet of buoyant 4-inch hose deployed on a maritime pre-positioning ship in MPF operations, which delivers potable water to the high water mark and water storage locations. **Production capacity can range from 75 gallons per hour to as high as 3,000 gallons per hour per purification unit or system.** See Figure VI-3 for water production capabilities of selected purification systems.

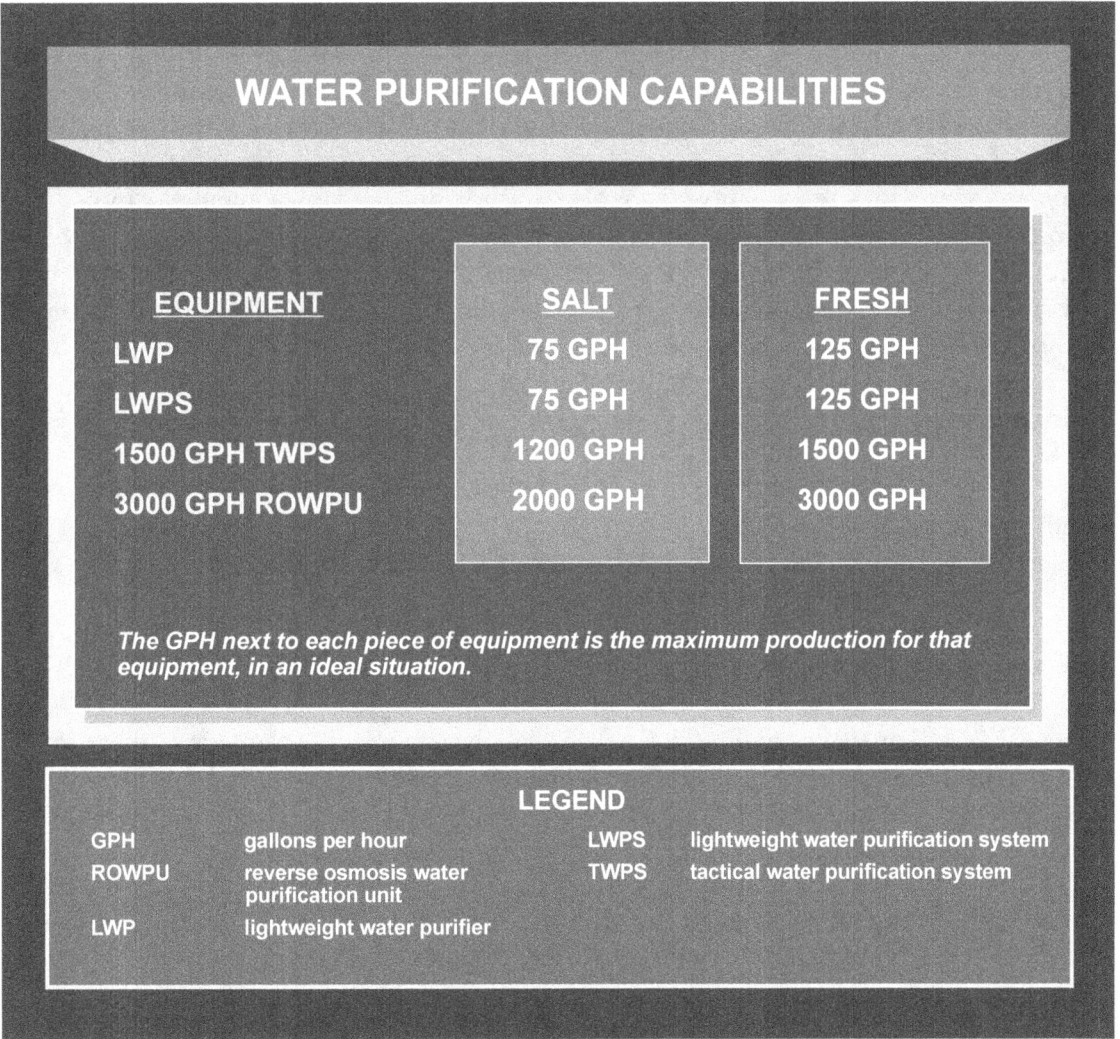

WATER PURIFICATION CAPABILITIES

EQUIPMENT	SALT	FRESH
LWP	75 GPH	125 GPH
LWPS	75 GPH	125 GPH
1500 GPH TWPS	1200 GPH	1500 GPH
3000 GPH ROWPU	2000 GPH	3000 GPH

The GPH next to each piece of equipment is the maximum production for that equipment, in an ideal situation.

LEGEND

GPH	gallons per hour	LWPS	lightweight water purification system
ROWPU	reverse osmosis water purification unit	TWPS	tactical water purification system
LWP	lightweight water purifier		

Figure VI-3. Water Purification Capabilities

b. **Phase II, Water Storage.** Water storage is the second phase of water support operations. Storage is normally done at or very close to the purification sites. The goal of water storage is to keep a sufficient quantity on hand to prevent a water shortage if several purification units become non-operational at one time. All storage of water will be in certified and approved containers. Normally, it will be done using 3,000, 20,000, and 50,000-gallon collapsible fabric tanks. Water distribution begins from the storage site.

c. **Phase III, Water Distribution. Water distribution often is the critical link in water support operations.** It is important that units organize so they will have sufficient organic water distribution equipment to provide supply point distribution. Units must have enough water distribution capacity to supply minimum requirements for water while making only one trip to the water point per day. During the early phases of deployments and in emergency situations, packaged water will be the primary means of resupply in forward areas. Once established, forces will use organic water distribution assets, such as tactical water distribution systems, Hippos, forward area water point supply systems, or water trailers.

d. **Other considerations.** Planners should maximize the use of HN sources if possible. **Water planners should assume no HN potable water is available in arid regions.** Minimal water sources and poor water quality may limit any operations that depend on HNS to meet the criteria set forth in Technical Bulletin Medical 577/Naval Medical Command P-5010-10/Air Force Manual 48-138, *Sanitary Control and Surveillance of Field Water Supplies,* (Army) for water quality standards. The potential exists for chemical, biological, and radiological attacks as well as conventional attacks on joint water distribution systems. Therefore, it is prudent for the unit to use a residual disinfectant and conduct a vulnerability assessment as soon as practical after arrival in theater. **In the early stages of deployment, HN processed or bottled water may be used if it has been certified as potable by preventive medicine personnel.** However, in theaters, JFCs and planners must be aware of the following:

(1) **Food and Water Supply.** Though the United States is not a party to Protocol I to the Geneva Conventions, the US adheres to many of its principles. For instance, Article 54 of Protocol I to the Geneva Conventions prohibits attacking, destroying, or rendering useless drinking water installations and supplies and irrigation works. In no event shall actions against these objects be taken that may be expected to leave the civilian population with such inadequate food or water as to cause its starvation or force its movement.

(2) **Labor force personnel.** The HN and theater contractor provided water support must provide for the needs of its labor forces unless otherwise provided in HNS agreements. In the absence of an agreement, US forces may have to assume some responsibility for the care of labor forces.

(3) **Refugees.** The Geneva Convention relative to the Protection of Civilian Persons in Time of War, of 12 August 1949, states that the host country, as the territorial sovereign, is responsible for refugees on its territory. In the event the host country's resources are strained by an influx of refugees, the host country may request assistance from other forces. If the host country is occupied by a hostile force, the occupying force is

responsible for ensuring public order and safety. Therefore, US forces may have responsibility to provide refugee care where they have occupied enemy territory.

(4) **Detainees.** The US is obliged to provide humane treatment to all persons in its custody (including prisoners of war and other types of detainee). This extends to providing sufficient water.

Intentionally Blank

APPENDIX A
PLANNING GUIDANCE FOR APPENDIX 1 TO ANNEX D, BULK PETROLEUM SUPPLY FOR MILITARY PLANS

1. Purpose

To provide guidance and formatting for use in the preparation of the bulk petroleum supply appendix of OPLANs and CONPLANs.

2. General

The bulk petroleum supply appendix to the logistic annex should include sufficient information to identify the consumption planning factors, fuel levels, storage, distribution, and time phasing of bulk petroleum capabilities required to support the plan. In cases where finite bulk petroleum requirements have not yet been determined, time-phased estimates of bulk petroleum requirements and capabilities should be provided. Identify petroleum products and distribution capability on hand or readily available that can be used to satisfy requirements for the war reserve stockage and resupply period. Access to, and sourcing from, HN bulk petroleum stocks and distribution resources should be identified when viable.

APPENDIX 1 to ANNEX D
(Bulk Petroleum Supply Appendix)

CLASSIFICATION
HEADQUARTERS, XXXX-XX COMMAND
ADDRESS
DATE

APPENDIX 1 TO ANNEX D TO CDRXXXX (Title of Specific Plan) XXXX
BULK PETROLEUM SUPPLY

References: List documents specifically referred to in this plan element.

1. General

a. **Users.** Designate the users to be supported, including multinational forces and civilian requirements, where applicable. Identify the agreements whereby support for the non-US military users would be undertaken.

b. **Assumptions.** List assumptions applicable to this appendix (e.g., scope of reliance on theater support contracts and HNS).

2. Concept of Operations

a. Describe the concept of petroleum operations.

b. Synchronize the concept of support with the concept of petroleum operations.

c. Designate the priority of supply and effort by phase.

d. Designate lead Service or agency as applicable.

e. Specify the end state of each phase and link them to the conditions necessary to start the next phase.

f. Consider vulnerability of the petroleum system to conventional and CBRN attacks.

g. Phases of the concept of petroleum operations should mirror the phase of the concept of support. Include theater and other major storage locations, quantity of storage, major customers, and concept of resupply.

(1) Type fuel and additives. In particular, designate or reiterate the single fuel for the operation and specify how non-single fuels will be handled.

(2) Intertheater and intratheater distribution concepts.

(3) OPDS requirements.

(4) IPDS requirements.

(5) Consolidated cargo-capable tanker requirements.

(6) QA and QS.

(7) HNS agreements or augmentation.

(8) Determine theater support contract requirements.

(9) Engineer construction support required.

(10) Tactical petroleum equipment required.

(11) Other, as appropriate.

3. Responsibilities

Assign specific responsibilities of organizations involved in providing bulk petroleum support (e.g., JPO, component commands, SAPOs, DLA Energy, DLA, and CCMDs).

4. Limiting Factors

Describe limitations that could adversely affect petroleum supply operations, such as inadequate air and ocean terminal capacity, lack of storage facilities, poorly positioned storage, inadequate intratheater and intertheater distribution, inadequate in-theater stocks, lack of alternate facilities, inadequate engineer construction support, and similar logistic constraints.

5. Estimate of Bulk Petroleum Support Requirements

Refer to Tab A, if applicable. Describe methods used to compute the requirements if Service planning factors are not applicable or if unique factors are considered.

TAB A to APPENDIX 1 to ANNEX D
(Format, Estimate of Bulk Petroleum Support Requirements Tab)

CLASSIFICATION
HEADQUARTERS, XXXX-XX COMMAND
ADDRESS
DATE

TAB A TO APPENDIX 1 TO ANNEX D TO CDRXXX (Title of Specific Plan)
XXXX

ESTIMATE OF BULK PETROLEUM SUPPORT REQUIREMENTS								
Estimated Consumption (M Barrels)*								
Product**	Service	C+C9	C+C10-19	C+C20-29	C+C30-39	C+C40-49	C+C50-59	C+C60-89
JP8	USA							
	USN MSC							
	USAF CRAF							
	USMC							
	TOTAL							

*1 M Barrel = 1,000 barrels
** One product per table

10-day increments for the first 60 days. Stop at C+89 (90 days). NATO 7-day increment format for first 45 days can be used vice 10-day format.

CLASSIFIED BY: _____
REASON: _____
DECLASSIFY BY: _____

Figure A-1. Estimate of Bulk Petroleum Support Requirements

Intentionally Blank

APPENDIX B
PLANNING GUIDANCE FOR APPENDIX 2 TO ANNEX D, WATER PURIFICATION AND DISTRIBUTION FOR OPERATION PLANS

1. Purpose

To provide guidance and formatting for use in the preparation of the water purification and distribution appendix of OPLANs and CONPLANs.

2. General

The water purification and distribution appendix to the logistic annex should include sufficient information to identify the consumption planning factors, storage, distribution, and time-phasing of water capabilities required to support the plan. In cases where finite water requirements have not yet been determined, time-phased estimates of water requirements and capabilities should be provided. Identify water purification and distribution capability on hand or readily available that can be used to satisfy requirements for the wartime tasking. Access to, and sourcing from, HN water and distribution resources should be identified when viable.

APPENDIX 2 to ANNEX D
(Format, Water Purification, and Distribution Appendix)

CLASSIFICATION
HEADQUARTERS, XXXX-XX COMMAND
ADDRESS
DATE

APPENDIX 2 TO ANNEX D TO CDRXXX (Title of Specific Plan) XXXX
WATER SUPPLY

References: List documents specifically referred to in this plan element.

1. General

a. **Users.** Designate the users to be supported, including multinational forces and civilian requirements, where applicable. Identify the agreements whereby support for the non-US military users would be undertaken.

b. **Assumptions.** List assumptions applicable to this appendix (e.g., scope of reliance on theater support contracts and HNS).

2. Concept of Operations

a. Describe the concept of water operations.

b. Synchronize the concept of support with the concept of water supply operations.

c. Designate the priority of supply and effort by phase.

d. Designate lead Service or agency as applicable.

e. Specify the end state of each phase and link them to the conditions necessary to start the next phase.

f. Consider vulnerability of the water system to terrorist, CBRN, and conventional attacks, and non-hostile source and distribution system deficiencies.

g. Phases of the concept of water supply operations should mirror the phase of the concept of support. Include the following:

    (1) Intertheater and intratheater distribution concepts.

    (2) Purification equipment requirements.

    (3) Distribution system requirements.

    (4) QA and QS.

    (5) HNS agreements or augmentation.

    (6) Engineer construction support required.

    (7) Tactical water equipment required.

    (8) Other, as appropriate.

3. Responsibilities

Assign specific responsibilities of organizations involved in providing water support (e.g., component commands and CCMDs).

4. Limiting Factors

Describe limitations that could adversely affect water supply operations, such as inadequate water source, lack of storage facilities, poorly positioned storage, inadequate intratheater and intertheater distribution, lack of equipment, lack of transportation assets, and similar logistic constraints.

5. Estimate of Water Support Requirements

Refer to Tab A, if applicable. Describe methods used to compute the requirements if Service planning factors are not applicable or if unique factors are considered.

TAB A to APPENDIX 2 to ANNEX D
(Format, Estimate of Water Support Requirements Tab)

CLASSIFICATION
HEADQUARTERS, XXXX-XX COMMAND
ADDRESS
DATE

TAB A TO APPENDIX 2 TO ANNEX D TO CDRXXX (Title of Specific Plan)
XXXX

ESTIMATE OF WATER SUPPORT REQUIREMENTS								
Estimated Consumption (In Gallons)								
Product	Service	C+C9	C+C10-19	C+C20-29	C+C30-39	C+C40-49	C+C50-59	C+C60-89
Water	USA							
	USN MSC							
	USAF CRAF							
	USMC							
	TOTAL							

10-day increments for the first 60 days. Stop at C+89 (90 days). NATO 7-day increment format for first 45 days can be used vice 10-day format.

CLASSIFIED BY: _____
REASON: _____
DECLASSIFY ON: _____

Figure B-1. Estimate of Water Support Requirements

Intentionally Blank

APPENDIX C
PETROLEUM SCENARIO

This appendix provides a notional petroleum scenario featuring items a JPO would do at the start of a contingency.

1. **Situation.** You are the joint petroleum officer for United States Africa Command (USAFRICOM). You have just been notified that an operation is being planned for the country of Wanda. Details of the operation are below. The purpose of this scenario is for potential or current JPO personnel to become familiar with the steps required to plan for and execute the early days of a contingency.

2. **Mission.** The Secretary of Defense, by order of the President of the United States, directs the Commander, United States Africa Command (CDRUSAFRICOM), to plan for and accomplish a humanitarian assistance mission to the country of Wanda, Africa. US forces will assist the Wanda military forces and OGAs, IGOs, and NGOs in accomplishment of this mission. It is anticipated that other nations will join this effort; however, the extent and timing of this assistance is uncertain. The US forces to be involved in this operation include US Air Force (one force projection wing and required transport aircraft), US Army (two brigades of the 82nd Airborne Division and appropriate support elements), and US Marine Corps (one Marine expeditionary brigade). The Army is the lead service for providing common item support to this operation to include petroleum support.

The CDRUSAFRICOM has the predominant fuels responsibility within a theater, and this responsibility will be discharged by the JPO. The USAFRICOM JPO works in conjunction with its Service components, the SAPO (as appointed) for the Wanda area, and DLA Energy to plan, coordinate, and oversee all phases of bulk petroleum support for US forces employed or planned for possible employment in the theater. The JPO will have a mix of Service representatives. Operational requirements dictate the establishment of SAPOs in support of subordinate JFCs. However, consideration will be given to the JOA and expected mission support, force composition, and sustainment requirements when selecting SAPOs.

3. **Background.** The Republic of Wanda is a small landlocked country in the Great Lakes region of east-central Africa, bordered by Ganda, Urundi, the Democratic Republic of the Ongo, and Zana. Home to approximately 10.1 million people, Wanda supports the densest population in continental Africa, most of whom engage in subsistence agriculture. A verdant country of fertile and hilly terrain, the small republic bears the title "Land of Many Valleys."

4. **Geography**

   a. The high altitude of Wanda provides the country with a pleasant tropical highland climate, with a mean daily temperature range of less than 2° Celsius (C) (36° Fahrenheit [F]). Temperatures vary considerably from region to region because of the variations in altitude. At Gali, on the central plateau, the average temperature is 21° C (70° F). Rainfall is heaviest in the southwest and lightest in the east. A long rainy season lasts from February to May and a short one from November through December. In the west, near Zenbuye, annual rainfall

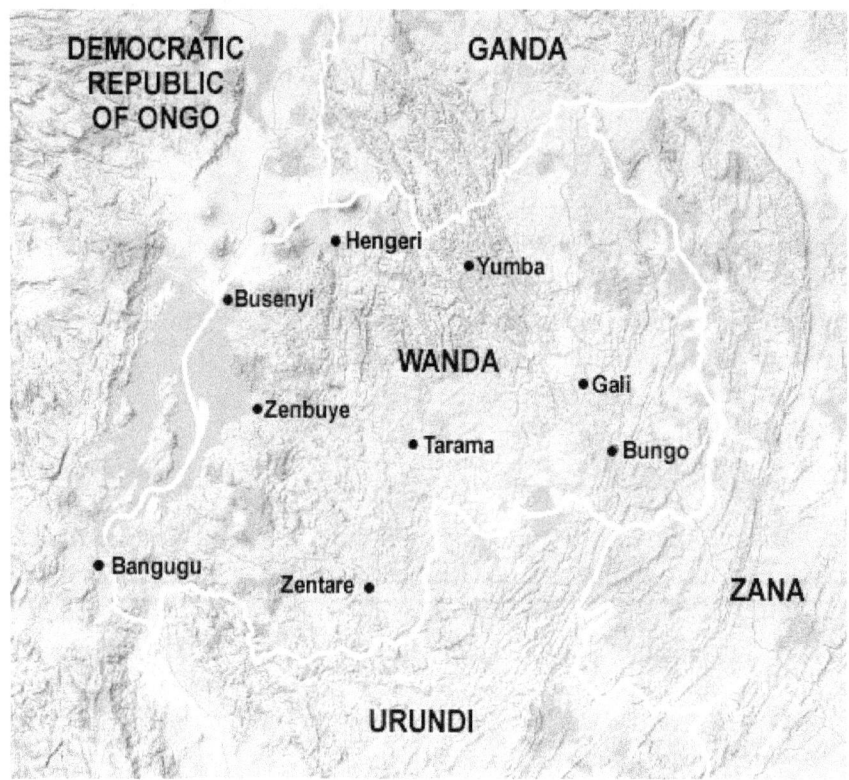

averages 160 centimeters (cm) (63 inches [in]); in the northeast, 78 cm (31 in); and at Zentare, in the south, 115 cm (45 in).

b. Wanda has been characterized by significant civil and political unrest for the past 50 years. This unrest, coupled with living conditions, has resulted in the loss of an estimated one million lives during this time. The infrastructure in the nation has not kept pace with the population growth and demands and has contributed to significant shortages of water and food and medical care. Recent events have highlighted the severity of the situation and led to the President ordering the humanitarian action.

5. Petroleum

Marketing. Distribution and marketing of fuels products is carried out by ERP (Enterprise Wandaise de Petrole), SGP (Societe Generale de Petrole), Wanda Petrolgaz, PetroWanda (bought out by Atlantic Gas in June 1999), Western Oil (acquired by Genco in July 2000), and Atlantic Gas. ERP, SGP, and Wanda Petrolgaz are privately owned companies while the government had a major shareholding in PetroWanda.

6. Petroleum Companies – Location

Western Oil Wanda SARL

Western Oil Wanda

Genco Petroleum, Wanda

Enterprise Wandaise de Petrole

PetroWanda

Wanda Petrolgaz

Societe Generale de Petrole

ERP has the largest market share, followed by PetroWanda (now Atlantic Gas). There is no restriction regarding the importation of petroleum products.

In June 1999, Atlantic Gas took over PetroWanda for US$2.1million. At the time of purchase, the company had more liabilities than assets. This constitutes part of the Wandan government's drive toward a massive privatization program. In July 2000, the South African company Genco acquired the marketing and distribution activities of Western Oil in Wanda and Urundi.

7. Distribution and Storage

a. Being landlocked, the country depends on road, rail, or air transport, although pipelines are used for moving large volumes of petroleum. The main supply route runs from the Mombasa refinery to Nairobi in Kenya by a 485 kilometers (km) pipeline and on to Gali via Ganda by tank trucks along a 1,250 km road route. Alternative routes exist from Nairobi to Tanzania; Dar-es-Salaam to Gali; or by rail from Dar-es-Salaam to Tabora and Isaka and then by road from Isaka to Gali (600 km). Because of high transport costs, insecurity of supply, and low-income levels; the population relies heavily on traditional fuels such as fuelwood, charcoal, and agricultural by-products, which account for 90 percent of the country's energy requirements.

b. The oil companies are required to keep 10,000 cubic meters of operational stock to ensure that there is sufficient petroleum supply within the country. Storage facilities are located at: Gali, Busenyi, Hengeri, and Zentare. There are three facilities of 3,660 cubic meters each at Hengeri and two facilities of 1,950 cubic meters at Zentare.

8. Pricing

The price of gasoline and diesel is fixed by the government while other petroleum products are not controlled. The government's oil price policy is used to keep the selling price constant while adapting the level of taxation to compensate for changes in the world market. The tax content of the selling price of gasoline is 44 percent and of diesel 46 percent. Kerosene is taxed at 6.2 percent and fuel oil at 14.6 percent. The tax content includes a road fund tax.

9. **Wandan Airports**

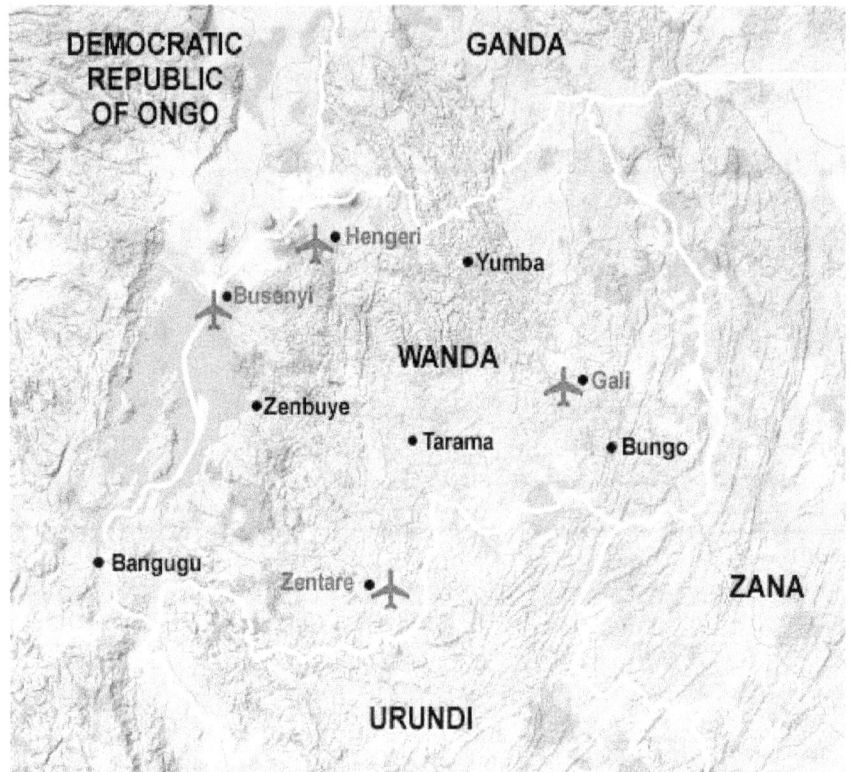

10. **Solution**

a. The CDRUSAFRICOM has the predominant fuels responsibility within the theater, and this responsibility is discharged by the JPO. The JPO works in conjunction with its Service components, SAPOs, and DLA Energy to plan, coordinate, and oversee all phases of bulk petroleum support for US forces employed or planned for possible employment in the theater.

b. One of the early tasks of the JPO is to establish the lead Service or agency responsible for bulk petroleum support for this joint operation. Since the Army is going to have a major force on the ground and normally is tasked with the inland distribution of bulk petroleum the JPO determines that the Army should be designated as the lead service for bulk petroleum.

c. Additionally, as a part of this effort, DLA Energy is asked to provide planning and information resources for use in this operation. Items that are most important are as follows:

    (1) Availability of fuel from commercial sources,

    (2) Timeline for the provision of fuel,

    (3) Availability of commercial transportation,

    (4) Timeline for the availability of commercial transportation,

(5) Amount of fuel that can be transported per day, by each transport mode (pipeline, truck, etc.), and

(6) Availability of commercial storage—where, how much, when can it be available.

d. This should include the appropriate contracting resources so contracts for local fuel, equipment, storage, quality support can be established quickly.

e. The JPO requests an in-country team of petroleum experts be deployed to Wanda very early in the deployment. This team includes DLA Energy, the components, especially the Army, and perhaps some civilian experts. The JPO discusses with DLA Energy if that team should report directly to DLA Energy or should it be under the operational control of the JPO. Provisions are made for the administrative and life support for the team to include transportation.

f. The next major task the JPO undertakes is to provide petroleum logistic planning and policy guidance to the component commanders. This is not an easy task given the isolated location of Wanda and the apparent scarcity of petroleum resources. Major issues that are a top priority for information gathering are as follows:

(1) Each component is asked to do a projection of daily fuel requirements for the first 30 days of the operation.

(2) The JPO validates the component bulk petroleum requirements, as much as feasible.

(3) The bulk petroleum requirements are shared with DLA Energy planners and the lead for the Army. This is the basis for a considerable amount of the preplanning prior to the deployment.

(4) The JPO considers the support that might be required for the support of the OGAs, IGOs, and NGOs in accomplishment of this mission. Requirements are solicited from these organizations.

(5) The JPO must consider that at some time in the future support might be necessary for forces from other nations who will join this effort even though the extent and timing of this assistance is uncertain. Since a tentative list of possible nations exists, the JPO starts to coordinate and negotiate multinational petroleum support.

(6) The JPO determines if there are any existing DLA Energy contracts in the area.

(7) Additionally, the JPO researches what available contracts are there in adjacent counties or theaters to support this contingency.

(8) Furthermore, the JPO identifies commercial resources (such as fuel, transportation, storage, and quality testing) available that might be put under DLA Energy contract.

(9) The JPO ascertains what theater war reserves are available for use. The release or reallocation of these resources are addressed in the OPLANs.

(10) Based on the answers and research on the preceding, the JPO requests that components estimate what tactical equipment must be sent into Wanda to support the operation.

(11) Based on the preceding fuel availability estimate, the JPO coordinates with DLA Energy to establish contracts in Wanda for fuel. DLA Energy also looks at adjacent countries for fuel and transportation assets that could be contracted for to support the operation.

(12) The JPO additionally inquires what, if any, Wanda government or military resources are available that might be made available through an HNS contract or other agreement.

(13) Coordination with the Air Force component and USTRANSCOM is accomplished to determine the stationing and refuel plan for transport and other aircraft. Since it would appear fuel resources in Wanda will be limited, aircraft flow is organized in such a manner so use of in-country fuel is limited.

(14) Based on information above the JPO looks at what fuel assets are necessary to be moved by air (aerial refuelers, bladder birds, etc.) to support the initial stages of the operation.

g. The JPO contacts the American Embassy in-country team to explore possible HNS. If some is available, the appropriate organization should negotiate, in coordination with DLA Energy, formal HNS agreements. This includes fuel and equipment in adjacent countries that might be transported into Wanda or used in support of the Wanda operation.

h. The JPO begins coordination and discussion with DLA Energy regarding the amount of contract fuel support that could be available/needed in the operation.

i. Based on the initial estimates of contract support availability the JPO provides the components with the amount of military support that would be necessary. This includes fuel, equipment, transport, and personnel. The JPO directs the tactical movement of fuels by means available to components in the theater.

j. The JPO coordinates the unique capabilities of each service with the joint planners. This becomes part of the bulk petroleum annex of the OPLANs.

k. The JPO integrates and applies the threat assessments and force protection measures in petroleum planning and operations. Special emphasis should be placed on ensuring adequate convoy protection, personnel protection, and protection of facilities.

l. The JPO ensures the preceding information is used to develop fuel requirements, operations, and constraints are addressed in the bulk petroleum annex of the OPLANs.

m. The JPO plans and coordinates the receipt, storage, and distribution of petroleum products in coordination with DLA Energy and the Service component commanders.

n. The JPO ensures the components and DLA Energy have a robust QS program.

o. The JPO makes an early assessment on the desirability of having a SAPO in the country of Wanda. Because of the span of control and data gathering and execution required, the JPO requests the GCC to appoint a SAPO with appropriate staff to fulfill bulk petroleum planning and execution matters in a section of the theater for which the JPO is responsible. The JPO considers the establishment of more than one SAPO in the theater. The SAPOs are normally required to:

(1) Conform to the administrative and technical procedures established by the CCDR and DOD 4140.25-M, *DOD Management of Bulk Petroleum Products, Natural Gas, and Coal.*

(2) Be under the operational control of the JFC (if there is one).

p. The key duties and responsibilities outlined for the SAPO are to:

(1) Advise the JFC and staff on petroleum logistic planning and policy and provide to Service components and commands the JFC's petroleum logistic planning and policy.

(2) Prepare directives concerning the management, accountability, operation, and QA of petroleum activities in the JOA.

(3) Prepare petroleum input for JFC supporting plans and develop daily demand profiles and petroleum supply and distribution plans for OPLANs/OPORDs. State bulk petroleum requirements through the CCMD JPO to DLA Energy to obtain sourcing from DOD stocks, local commercial, or host government resources using DLA Energy contractual coverage or service/country fuel agreements.

(4) Establish a direct LOC with the CCMD JPO concerning all aspects of petroleum activities.

(5) State bulk petroleum requirements through the CCMD JPO to DLA Energy to obtain sourcing from DOD stocks, local commercial, or host government resources using DLA Energy contractual coverage or service/country fuel agreements.

(6) Submit REPOL petroleum damage and deficiency report as required to the CCMD JPO.

(7) Assign JFC priorities and advise the CCMD JPO and DLA Energy for construction projects, maintenance, and repair projects for petroleum facilities.

(8) Validate existing quantity and quality of local inventories, estimated DOS on hand, and method and quantity of daily resupply capability by product.

(9) Coordinate and advise the CCMD JPO concerning local petroleum capabilities.

(10) Establish JFC requirements/coordinate with the JPO and DLA Energy for leased storage and related activities in the JOA.

(11) Coordinate with local commercial and host government to determine availability of commodity and capability to support bulk petroleum operational requirements.

(12) Identify/submit requirements IAW current HNS agreements to the HN for HN petroleum support.

(13) Supervise bulk petroleum operations. Coordinate with commercial sources and host governments for the use of tanker loading/off-loading facilities.

(14) Coordinate with the DLA Energy, CCMD JPO, and service component bulk petroleum managers to maintain visibility of bulk petroleum operations.

(15) Maintain operational petroleum delivery requirements from Service component petroleum, oils, and lubricants managers to maintain visibility of bulk petroleum operations.

(16) Maintain operational petroleum delivery requirements from Service component petroleum managers.

(17) Consolidate component delivery requirements and forward them to DLA Energy.

(18) Coordinate QS and procurement inspection programs.

(19) Advise the JFC, under emergency conditions, on the allocation of petroleum, oils, and lubricants and facilities and coordinate with component control points.

(20) Release or reallocate JOA PWRS.

(21) Notify the J-4 and CCMD JPO when PWRS will be penetrated and provide a plan for reconstitution of levels including a time frame when levels will be covered.

(22) Maintain thorough knowledge and understanding of JFC OPLANs/OPORDs and component and supporting forces CONOPS/support.

(23) Coordinate allocation and construction of inland petroleum distribution system assets.

(24) Provide broad guidance and supervision to the SAPO members.

q. With the proper consideration of planning factors, the establishment of roles and offices, and the coordination underway with components and SAPOs, the JPO is now ready to commence successful operations.

APPENDIX D
REFERENCES

The development of JP 4-03 is based upon the following primary references:

1. Department of Defense Publications

    a. DODD 4140.25, *DOD Management Policy for Energy Commodities and Related Service.*

    b. DODD 4705.1, *Management of Land-Based Water Resources in Support of Contingency Operations.*

    c. DODD 5101.8, *Department of Defense (DOD) Executive Agent (EA) for Bulk Petroleum.*

    d. DODD 5530.3, *International Agreements.*

    e. DODI 3110.6, *War Reserve Materiel Policy.*

    f. DODI 4715.05, *Overseas Environmental Compliance.*

    g. DODI 4715.5, *Management of Environmental Compliance at Overseas Installations.*

    h. DOD 4140.25-M, *DOD Management of Bulk Petroleum Products, Natural Gas, and Coal.*

    i. DOD 4715.5-G, *Overseas Environmental Baseline Guidance Document.*

2. Chairman of the Joint Chiefs of Staff Publications

    a. CJCSI 3110.01G, *Joint Strategic Capabilities Plan FY2008.*

    b. CJCSM 3122.03C, *Joint Operation Planning and Execution System Volume II, Planning Formats.*

    c. CJCSM 3150.14B, *Joint Reporting Structure (JRS), Logistics.*

    d. CJCSI 3150.25D, *Joint Lessons Learned Program (JLLP).*

    e. JP 3-28, *Civil Support.*

    f. JP 4-0, *Joint Logistics.*

    g. JP 4-01.6, *Joint Logistics Over-the-Shore (JLOTS).*

    h. JP 4-07, *Common-User Logistics During Joint Operations.*

    i. JP 4-08, *Logistic Support of Multinational Operations.*

3. Other Publications

    a. *Joint Petroleum Logistics Planning Guide, June 2003.*

    b. MIL-STD-3004, *Quality Assurance/Surveillance for Fuels, Lubricants, and Related Products.*

    c. Defense Energy Support Center-Environmental Guide Fuel Terminal.

    d. DLA Memorandum to DESC, 1 November 2004.

APPENDIX E
ADMINISTRATIVE INSTRUCTIONS

1. User Comments

Users in the field are highly encouraged to submit comments on this publication to: Commander, United States Joint Forces Command, Joint Warfighting Center, ATTN: Doctrine and Education Group, 116 Lake View Parkway, Suffolk, VA 23435-2697. These comments should address content (accuracy, usefulness, consistency, and organization), writing, and appearance.

2. Authorship

The lead agent and Joint Staff doctrine sponsor for this publication is the J-4.

3. Supersession

This publication supersedes JP 4-03, 23 May 2003, *Joint Bulk Petroleum and Water Doctrine*.

4. Change Recommendations

a. Recommendations for urgent changes to this publication should be submitted electronically to the Joint Staff J-4, with information copies sent to the Joint Staff J-7 Joint Doctrine and Education Division and to the US Joint Forces Command J-7/Joint Warfighting Center, Doctrine and Education Group.

```
TO:     JOINT STAFF WASHINGTON DC//J4/J7-JDETD//
INFO:   JOINT STAFF WASHINGTON DC//J7-JEDD//CDRUSJFCOM
        SUFFOLK VA//JT10//
```

b. Routine changes should be submitted electronically to the US Joint Forces Command Joint J-7/Joint Warfighting Center, Doctrine and Education Group, and info the Joint Staff J-4 and the Joint Staff J-7 Joint Doctrine and Education Division.

c. When a Joint Staff directorate submits a proposal to the Chairman of the Joint Chiefs of Staff that would change source document information reflected in this publication, that directorate will include a proposed change to this publication as an enclosure to its proposal. The Military Services and other organizations are requested to notify the Joint Staff J-7 when changes to source documents reflected in this publication are initiated.

d. Record of Changes:

CHANGE NUMBER	COPY NUMBER	DATE OF CHANGE	DATE ENTERED	POSTED BY	REMARKS

5. Distribution of Publications

Local reproduction is authorized and access to unclassified publications is unrestricted. However, access to and reproduction authorization for classified joint publications must be in accordance with DOD 5200.1-R, *Information Security Program.*

6. Distribution of Electronic Publications

a. Joint Staff J-7 will not print copies of JPs for distribution. Electronic versions are available on JDEIS at https://jdeis.js.mil (NIPRNET), and https://jdeis.js.smil.mil (SIPRNET) and on the JEL at http://www.dtic.mil/doctrine (NIPRNET).

b. Only approved JPs and joint test publications are releasable outside the combatant commands, Services, and Joint Staff. Release of any classified JP to foreign governments or foreign nationals must be requested through the local embassy (Defense Attaché Office) to DIA, Defense Foreign Liaison/IE-3, 200 MacDill Blvd., Bolling AFB, Washington, DC 20340-5100.

c. CD-ROM. Upon request of a JDDC member, the Joint Staff J-7 will produce and deliver one CD-ROM with current JPs.

GLOSSARY
PART I—ABBREVIATIONS AND ACRONYMS

ABFDS	aerial bulk fuel delivery system
ACSA	acquisition and cross-servicing agreement
AIK	assistance in kind
AMC	Air Mobility Command
AOR	area of responsibility
BPA	blanket purchase agreement
CBRN	chemical, biological, radiological, and nuclear
CCDR	combatant commander
CCMD	combatant command
CDRUSAFRICOM	Commander, United States Africa Command
CJCSM	Chairman of the Joint Chiefs of Staff manual
CONPLAN	concept plan
CONOPS	concept of operations
COP	common operational picture
COR	contracting officer representative
CSA	combat support agency
DFSP	defense fuel support point
DLA	Defense Logistics Agency
DOD	Department of Defense
DODD	Department of Defense directive
DODI	Department of Defense instruction
DOS	days of supply
EA	executive agent
FAR	Federal Acquisition Regulation
FGS	final governing standard
FOO	field ordering officer
FORCE	fuels operational readiness capability equipment (Air Force)
GCC	geographic combatant commander
HN	host nation
HNS	host-nation support
HQ	headquarters
IAW	in accordance with
ICIS	integrated consumable item support
IGO	intergovernmental organization

IMM	integrated materiel management
IMP	inventory management plan
IPDP	inland petroleum distribution plan
IPDS	inland petroleum distribution system (Army)
J-4	logistics directorate of a joint staff
JARB	joint acquisition review board
JCS	Joint Chiefs of Staff
JFC	joint force commander
JLE	joint logistics environment
JLOTS	joint logistics over-the-shore
JMPAB	Joint Materiel Priorities and Allocation Board
JOA	joint operations area
JP	joint publication
JPO	joint petroleum office
JSCP	Joint Strategic Capabilities Plan
LN	lead nation
LOC	line of communications
LSA	logistics supportability analysis
MILCON	military construction
MILSPEC	military specification
MIL-STD	military standard
MNF	multinational force
MPF	maritime pre-positioning force
MSC	Military Sealift Command
NATO	North Atlantic Treaty Organization
NGO	nongovernmental organization
OGA	other government agency
OPDS	offshore petroleum discharge system
OPLAN	operation plan
OPORD	operation order
OSD	Office of the Secretary of Defense
PC&S	post, camp, and station
POLCAP	bulk petroleum capabilities report
POS	peacetime operating stocks
PWRR	petroleum war reserve requirements
PWRS	pre-positioned war reserve stock
QA	quality assurance
QS	quality surveillance
REPOL	bulk petroleum contingency report

SAPO	subarea petroleum office
SCP	service control point
SFC	single-fuel concept
S/RM	sustainment, restoration, and modernization
TPFDD	time-phased force and deployment data
TSC	theater sustainment command (Army)
ULSD	ultra-low sulfur diesel
USAFRICOM	United States Africa Command
USD(AT&L)	Under Secretary of Defense for Acquisition, Technology, and Logistics
USJFCOM	United States Joint Forces Command
USTRANSCOM	United States Transportation Command
WHNS	wartime host-nation support

PART II—TERMS AND DEFINITIONS

bin storage. None. (Approved for removal from JP 1-02.)

bulk petroleum product. A liquid petroleum product transported by various means and stored in tanks or containers having an individual fill capacity greater than 250 liters. (JP 1-02. SOURCE: JP 4-03)

bulk storage. 1. Storage in a warehouse of supplies and equipment in large quantities, usually in original containers, as distinguished from bin storage. 2. Storage of liquids, such as petroleum products in tanks, as distinguished from drum or packaged storage. (Approved for incorporation into JP 1-02.)

executive agent. A term used to indicate a delegation of authority by the Secretary of Defense to a subordinate to act on behalf of the Secretary of Defense. Designation as executive agent, in and of itself, confers no authority. The exact nature and scope of the authority delegated must be stated in the document designating the executive agent. An executive agent may be limited to providing only administration and support or coordinating common functions, or it may be delegated authority, direction, and control over specified resources for specified purposes. Also called **EA.** (JP 1-02. SOURCE: JP 1)

inland petroleum distribution system. A multi-product system consisting of both commercially available and military standard petroleum equipment that can be assembled by military personnel and, when assembled into an integrated petroleum distribution system, provides the military with the capability required to support an operational force with bulk fuels. The inland petroleum distribution system is comprised of three primary subsystems: tactical petroleum terminal, pipeline segments, and pump stations. Also called **IPDS.** (Approved for incorporation into JP 1-02.)

integrated consumable item support. A decision support system that takes time-phased force and deployment data (i.e., Department of Defense deployment plans) and calculates the ability of the Defense Logistics Agency, the warehousing unit of the Department of Defense, to support those plans. Integrated consumable item support can calculate for the planned deployment supply/demand curves for over two million individual items stocked by the Defense Logistics Agency in support of deployment. Also called **ICIS.** (Approved for replacement of "Integrated Consumable Item Support" and its definition in JP 1-02.)

integrated materiel management. The exercise of total Department of Defense-level management responsibility for a federal supply group or class, commodity, or item for a single agency. It normally includes computation of requirements, funding, budgeting, storing, issuing, cataloging, standardizing, and procuring functions. Also called **IMM.** (JP 1-02. SOURCE: JP 4-07)

lead nation. One nation assumes the responsibility for procuring and providing a broad spectrum of logistic support for all or a part of the multinational force and/or headquarters. Compensation and/or reimbursement will then be subject to agreements between the parties involved. The lead nation may also assume the responsibility to coordinate logistics of the other nations within its functional and regional area of responsibility. (JP 1-02. SOURCE: JP 4-0)

materiel readiness. The availability of materiel required by a military organization to support its wartime activities or contingencies, disaster relief (flood, earthquake, etc.), or other emergencies. (Approved for incorporation into JP 1-02 with JP 4-03 as the source JP.)

offshore petroleum discharge system. Provides bulk transfer of petroleum directly from an offshore tanker to a beach termination unit located immediately inland from the high watermark. Bulk petroleum then is either transported inland or stored in the beach support area. Also called **OPDS.** (Approved for incorporation into JP 1-02.)

peacetime operating stocks. Logistics resources on hand or on order necessary to support day-to-day operational requirements, and which, in part, can also be used to offset sustaining requirements. Also called **POS.** (JP 1-02. SOURCE: JP 4-03)

petroleum intersectional service. None. (Approved for removal from JP 1-02.)

receiving ship. Ship in a replenishment unit that receives the rig(s). (JP 1-02. SOURCE: JP 4-03)

role specialist nation. A nation that has agreed to assume responsibility for providing a particular class of supply or service for all or part of the multinational force. Also called **RSN.** (JP 1-02. SOURCE: JP 4-08)

sustainment, restoration, and modernization. The fuels asset sustainment program within Defense Energy Support Center that provides a long-term process to cost-effectively sustain, restore, and modernize fuel facilities. Also called **S/RM.** (Approved for inclusion in JP 1-02.)

tactical airfield fuel dispensing system. A tactical aircraft refueling system deployed by a Marine air-ground task force in support of air operations at an expeditionary airfield or a forward arming and refueling point. Also called **TAFDS.** (Approved for incorporation into JP 1-02 with JP 4-03 as the source JP.)

Intentionally Blank

JOINT DOCTRINE PUBLICATIONS HIERARCHY

			JP 1 **JOINT DOCTRINE**		

JP 1-0 **PERSONNEL**	JP 2-0 **INTELLIGENCE**	JP 3-0 **OPERATIONS**	JP 4-0 LOGISTICS	JP 5-0 **PLANS**	JP 6-0 **COMMUNICATION SYSTEMS**

All joint publications are organized into a comprehensive hierarchy as shown in the chart above. **Joint Publication (JP) 4-03** is in the Logistics series of joint doctrine publications. The diagram below illustrates an overview of the development process:

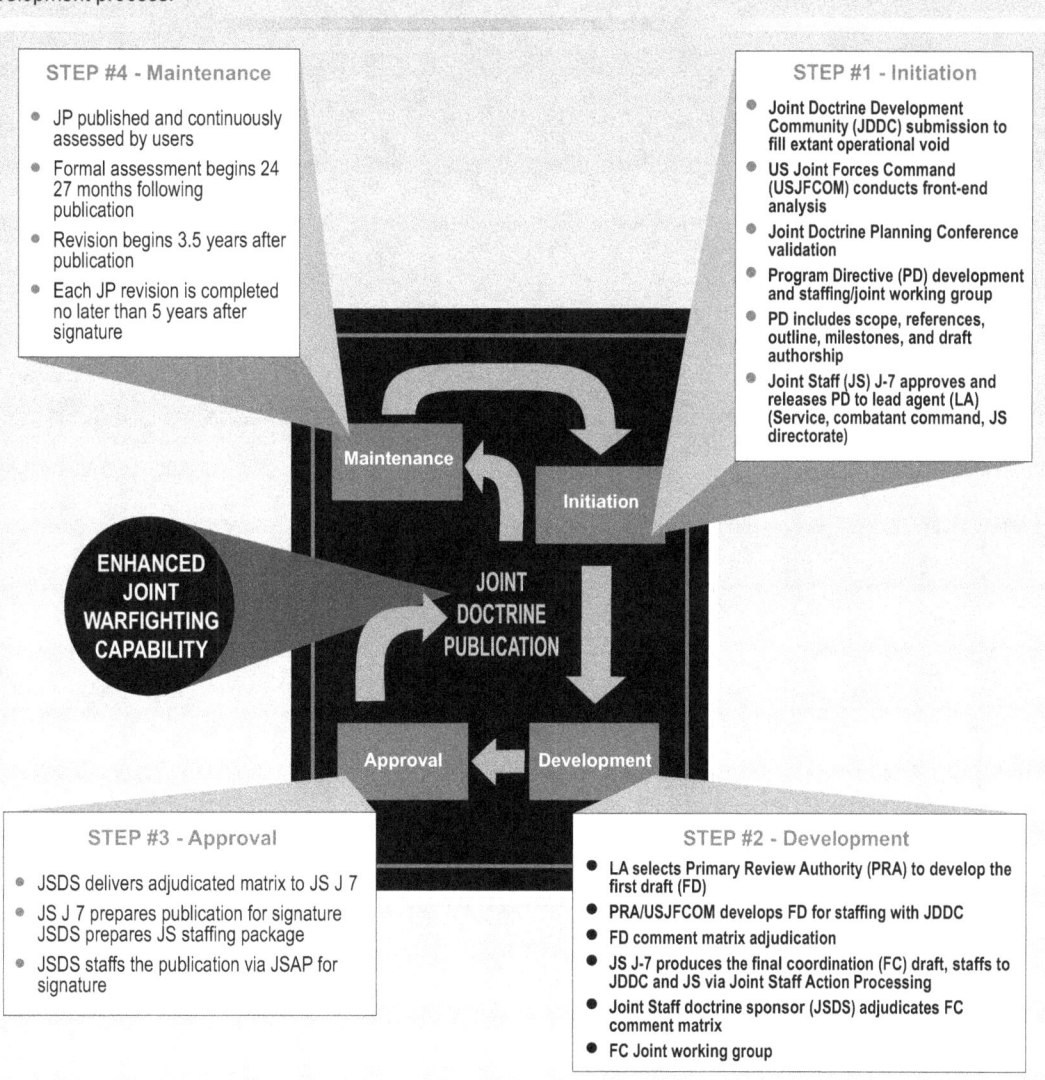

STEP #4 - Maintenance

- JP published and continuously assessed by users
- Formal assessment begins 24 27 months following publication
- Revision begins 3.5 years after publication
- Each JP revision is completed no later than 5 years after signature

STEP #1 - Initiation

- Joint Doctrine Development Community (JDDC) submission to fill extant operational void
- US Joint Forces Command (USJFCOM) conducts front-end analysis
- Joint Doctrine Planning Conference validation
- Program Directive (PD) development and staffing/joint working group
- PD includes scope, references, outline, milestones, and draft authorship
- Joint Staff (JS) J-7 approves and releases PD to lead agent (LA) (Service, combatant command, JS directorate)

STEP #3 - Approval

- JSDS delivers adjudicated matrix to JS J 7
- JS J 7 prepares publication for signature JSDS prepares JS staffing package
- JSDS staffs the publication via JSAP for signature

STEP #2 - Development

- LA selects Primary Review Authority (PRA) to develop the first draft (FD)
- PRA/USJFCOM develops FD for staffing with JDDC
- FD comment matrix adjudication
- JS J-7 produces the final coordination (FC) draft, staffs to JDDC and JS via Joint Staff Action Processing
- Joint Staff doctrine sponsor (JSDS) adjudicates FC comment matrix
- FC Joint working group

www.ingramcontent.com/pod-product-compliance
Lightning Source LLC
Chambersburg PA
CBHW081327310526
45789CB00018B/2470